MW00533051

THE SECRET
SECRET
OF
EXPERIENCING
CHRIST

WITNESS LEE

Living Stream Ministry
Anaheim, CA • www.lsm.org

First Edition, November 1986.

ISBN 978-0-87083-227-7

Published by

Living Stream Ministry
2431 W. La Palma Ave., Anaheim, CA 92801 U.S.A.
P. O. Box 2121, Anaheim, CA 92814 U.S.A.

Printed in the United States of America

10   11   12   13   14   15   /   10   9   8   7   6   5   4

CONTENTS

PREFACE

The first seven chapters of this book consist of messages given during a conference in Tokyo, Japan, in October of 1984. The last four chapters consist of messages given during a conference in Anaheim, California, in November of 1981. All of these messages concern the secret of experiencing Christ.

CHAPTER ONE

CHRIST—THE COMPLETE GOD

Scripture Reading: Rom. 9:5; Exo. 3:14-16; John 1:1, 4; Heb. 1:10; John 1:18; 3:16; 6:46; 16:27; 17:8; 5:43; 10:25; Isa. 9:6; John 10:30; 14:10, 11; 8:16, 29; 14:32; 3:3, 4; 5:26; 14:26; 1 Cor. 15:45b; 2 Cor. 3:17; Rev. 22:13; 1 John 1:1-2; Col. 2:2, 9

In this book we will see the secret of experiencing Christ. Christ is the focus, the center, of the entire Bible. The Bible unveils Him to us that we may experience Him. God's eternal plan depends upon Him. He is the central person, the central figure, in the Bible. As Christians, we must experience Him day by day. If in a particular day we do not experience Christ, that day is in vain. The Christian life is one of experiencing Christ at all times. If we would experience Christ, we need to see what is the secret of experiencing Him.

RECEIVING THE REVELATION
CONCERNING THE PERSON OF CHRIST

In order to experience Christ, we first need to receive the revelation concerning His Person. Both the Bible and the entire history of mankind tell us that Christ is a wonderful Person. In the six thousand year history of mankind there has never been a Person as wonderful as Christ. He is not only wonderful, but also mysterious. No historian can deny that in human history there was such a mysterious Person as Jesus Christ. Christ is mysterious because no one can tell where He came from and where He went. No historian can tell us where Jesus Christ is today. Yet He is believed in, exalted, worshipped, and praised by millions of His believers on this earth. Although none of them has ever seen Him with his eyes, all of His believers love Him and many would even die for Him (1 Pet. 1:8). Many have given their lives for this Christ. He is a mystery which no human words can explain.

To receive the revelation concerning Christ, we must come to the Bible. In the Bible human language is used to describe Christ. Although He is mysterious, divine, and spiritual, the Bible uses human words to tell us who He is.

THE COMPLETE GOD

First the Bible tells us that Christ is the complete God. Romans 9:5 says that "Christ...is over all, God blessed forever." In the entire universe there is only one God (Isa. 45:5; 1 Cor. 8:4; 1 Tim. 2:5). This unique God is real, true, and living. Christ Himself is this very God. Christ is the complete God, not merely a part of God.

The Self-existing and Ever-existing One— the Great I Am

The Bible shows us that this Christ who is God is self-existing and ever-existing (Exo. 3:14). He has no beginning and no ending. In the Old Testament His name is Jehovah (Exo. 3:15). The divine title Jehovah actually means "to exist." It is similar in meaning to the English verb "to be." Jesus Christ is Jehovah, the great I Am, the great To Be (John 8:24, 28, 58). In the past He was, in the present He is, and in the future He will be. Every visible thing will pass away, but Christ remains forever (Heb. 1:10-12). He is the unique To Be.

Jehovah, the Triune God— the Father, the Son, and the Spirit

Exodus 3:15-16 reveals that, as Jehovah, Christ is the Triune God. The term "Triune God" does not mean that there are three Gods. It means that the one unique God is triune; He is the three-one God. He is one, yet three, and three, yet one. He is one God as the Father, the Son, and the Spirit (Matt. 28:19). This is a mystery which we cannot explain. We cannot explain how one can be three and three can be one. Christ is the unique God, yet He is the Father, the Son, and the Spirit.

The Eternal Word, God Himself

John 1:1 says, "In the beginning was the Word, and the Word was with God, and the Word was God." In this verse Christ is revealed as the eternal Word, who is God Himself.

The Creator

The Bible also reveals that Christ is the Creator (John 1:3; Heb. 1:10). The universe is His creation (Col. 1:16). He created the heavens and the earth. He created billions of items in the universe, and He created mankind, including you and me.

The Son of God

Christ is God, and He is also the Son of God (John 1:18; 3:16). In the Bible the Son of God signifies God's expression. Even in a human sense, the son is always the father's expression. When you see a son you realize the face of the father. Christ as the Son of God is the expression of God.

Sent from the Father, and Coming from with the Father

In John 6:46 and 16:27 the Lord Jesus said that He was "from God," and in John 17:8 He prayed to the Father, "I came forth from You, and...You sent Me." The Greek word translated "from" in these verses is *para,* meaning "by the side of." The sense of this Greek word is not only "from," but "from with." The Lord is not only from God, but also with God. While He is from God, He is still with God (cf. John 8:16, 29; 16:32).

The New Testament tells us that the Son was sent by the Father and also from with the Father. This means that when the Father sent Him, He sent Him with the Father Himself. For example, I may send someone to you and come with him. When he is coming to you, I am coming to you with him. This illustrates the mysterious fact that when the Father sent the Son, He also came with the Son.

Coming and Working in the Father's Name, and Being Called the Eternal Father

The New Testament also tells us that the Son came in the Father's name (John 5:43). When the Son comes, He comes with the Father and in the Father's name. Eventually, when the Son comes, the Father comes. When we have the Son, we have both the Son and the Father. We have the Son with the Father.

Furthermore, after coming, the Son worked in the Father's name (John 10:25). He not only came in the Father's name, but also did all His work in the Father's name. For this reason Isaiah 9:6 tells us that His name is called the Eternal Father. Because the Son came in the name of the Father and worked in the name of the Father, He is called the Father.

The Son and the Father Being One

The New Testament tells us that the Son and the Father are one (John 10:30). Yes, the Son is the Son, and the Father is the Father. The Two are distinct, but They are not separate. In one sense, the Son and the Father are two, but in another sense the Son and the Father are one. We cannot understand this, but it is nevertheless a fact. We can never separate Christ from the Father, for He and the Father are one.

Coinhering with the Father

In John 14:10 and 11 the Lord told us that He is in the Father and the Father is in Him. In theological terms, this is referred to as coinherence. Coinherence means that two persons exist, or abide, in one another. The Son declared that He was in the Father and the Father was in Him. The Two coinhere; They abide in one another. This is beyond our understanding, but still it is a fact.

Having the Father Always with Him

The Bible tells us that the Father was always with the Son. While Christ was on this earth, He told people that the Father was always with Him and never left Him alone (John 8:16, 29; 16:32). In John 16:32 the Lord Jesus told His disciples that when the persecution came, they all would leave Him alone. However, although they would leave Him, He was not alone, because the Father was with Him. He was always in the Father, and the Father was in Him. Therefore, He was always with the Father, and the Father was with Him.

This knowledge helps us to experience Christ. When we experience Christ, we do not experience Him alone, but we experience Him with the Father. We experience Him with the Father in Him and with Him in the Father. This makes our experience of Christ very rich.

First John 2:23 tells us that when we confess the Son, we have the Father also. Therefore, when we have the Son, we have the Father also. To have the Father means that we possess Him and are now participating in Him. We are now enjoying, not the Son alone, but the Son with the Father.

The Giver and Sender of the Spirit

In the Triune Godhead there are the Father, the Son, and the Spirit. Thus far, based on the Bible, we have seen that the Son and the Father are one. When we have Him, we enjoy Him with the Father. At this point we need to see further that Christ is the Giver of the Spirit (John 3:34) and also the Sender of the Spirit (John 15:26).

John 15:26 says, "But when the Comforter comes, whom I will send to you from the Father, the Spirit of reality who proceeds from the Father, He will testify concerning Me." According to this verse, Christ sends the Spirit from the Father. However, we must point out again that the Greek preposition *para,* translated "from" twice in this verse, carries the sense of both from and with. Actually, the basic thought of this Greek preposition is "with." Therefore, it is correct to translate *para* in this verse as "with," indicating clearly that the Son will send the Spirit with the Father. The Lord's word in 15:26 does not mean that He will send the Spirit *and* the Father, but it means that He will send the Spirit *with* the Father. The Father always comes with the Spirit.

How wonderful that when Christ sent the Spirit, the Spirit proceeded from the Father and came with the Father. When Christ gives the Spirit and sends the Spirit to us, the

Spirit comes with the Father. If we read only John 15:26, it may seem that the Spirit comes with the Father, but not with the Son. But if we read John 15:26 carefully with 14:26, we can see not only that Christ sends the Spirit and the Spirit comes to us with the Father, but also that the Father sends the Spirit in the name of the Son. According to John 15:26, Christ sends the Spirit and the Spirit comes with the Father, and according to 14:26, the Father sends the Spirit in the name of the Son. When the Spirit is given, He is given with the Father, and the Father also gives the Spirit in the name of the Son.

After reading these two verses, you might ask, "Who sent the Spirit, the Son or the Father?" One verse, 15:26, says that the Son sent the Spirit, and the other, 14:26, that the Father sent the Spirit in the Son's name. Both the Son and the Father are the Sender. The Two send the same Spirit. The Son sent the Spirit with the Father, and the Father sent the Spirit in the Son's name. Eventually, when the Spirit comes, the Three all come, because the Spirit sent by the Son comes with the Father, and the Spirit sent by the Father comes in the name of the Son. Hence, when the Spirit is given, when the Spirit enters into us, we have not only the Spirit, but the Spirit with the Father in the Son's name.

Many have believed in the Lord Jesus and have received Him as their Savior. They realize that the Lord Jesus is in them, but because they may not be so zealous for the Lord, they feel that they do not have the Spirit. To them the Lord in whom they have believed and whom they have received is only the Savior, but not the Spirit. The Lord is only qualified to die for them on the cross, to redeem them, and to save them, but He cannot inspire them and make them zealous for Him. In their concept, they have Christ, but they do not have the Spirit. According to their thinking, the Spirit is outside of them, and they still need to receive the Spirit apart from Christ.

Actually, Christ is always with the Father, and the Father is always with the Spirit. The Three are distinct, but They are not separate. The Bible does not convey the thought that the Son is on the earth, the Father is in the heavens, and the

Spirit is like a dove in the air. It does not teach us that when we receive Christ into us, the Father remains on the throne in the heavens, and the Spirit is still waiting for us to open up to Him. On the contrary, especially in the Gospel of John we are told clearly that the Father is always with the Son, and the Spirit is always with the Father. When we have the Son, we have the Spirit with the Father. When we have One, we have all Three.

We need to realize that when we have the Lord Jesus within us, we have the Father, the Son, and the Spirit. Our God is triune. He is not three separate Persons, but one Triune God. The English word "triune" is composed of two Latin words, "tri," meaning three, and "une," meaning one. Our God is one, yet He is three; He is three, yet still one. When we have One, we have all Three.

When we have the Son, we have the Father, for the Father is with the Son. We also have the Spirit, for the Spirit comes with the Father. There is no need for us to attempt to receive the Spirit apart from the Father and the Son. We only need to pray, "Lord Jesus, thank You that You are in me. I do realize that the Spirit is with You, and the Father is also with You. When I have You, I have the Father, and I also have the Spirit."

If we check with our own experiences, we will realize that when we call on the name of the Lord Jesus, we have the Lord Jesus, we have the Spirit, and we also have the Father with the Son. This kind of experience may have caused us to wonder who was in us, the Father, the Son, or the Spirit. While we are praying, we may feel that the Son is within us. Then, in the next moment we may sense that the Father is within us, and then after another moment, that the Spirit is within us.

When I was young my spiritual vision was not so clear. While praying I often became bothered and stopped to think, "On whom should I call? Should I call on the Lord Jesus, or should I call Abba, Father, or should I call on the Holy Spirit?" According to my feeling, all Three were there with me. Three were there, yet these Three were one. When I called, "O Lord Jesus," the Father was there. When I called, "O Father," the

Lord Jesus was there. At times, because I did not have a clear vision, I called on all Three at the same time.

We should not be bothered, but feel free to pray, "Lord Jesus, I thank You. O Father, I worship You. O Holy Spirit, thank You that You are with me." There is nothing wrong with such a prayer, because the Three of the Trinity are not separate. They are three-one. Therefore, in Matthew 28:19 the Lord told the disciples to go and disciple the nations, baptizing them into the one name of the Father, and of the Son, and of the Holy Spirit.

If we have a clear vision, we will be able to avoid many complications. For example, some Christian groups feel that they should baptize people three times, once in the name of the Father, once in the name of the Son, and once in the name of the Holy Spirit. I would not criticize this practice or say that it is wrong. However, I do feel that it is somewhat complicating and bothering. We do not have three Gods, but one unique God. We do not worship three Gods, but one God who is triune, the Father, the Son, and the Spirit. Strictly speaking, therefore, there is no need to baptize people three times. One time is good enough. I say this to illustrate how we need a clear vision concerning the Person of Christ.

Our Christ is all-inclusive. He is the complete God, and our God is triune—the Father, the Son, and the Spirit. We do not have three Gods; we have only one God, who is the Father, the Son, and the Spirit. Hallelujah, this unique God is Christ! We need to realize that when we experience Him, we experience the Triune God. We not only experience Jesus Christ, but we experience the complete Triune God.

Becoming the Life-giving Spirit
in His Resurrection, and Being the Spirit

The Bible reveals that Christ went to the cross, died, was buried, and rose from the dead. In resurrection He became a life-giving Spirit (1 Cor. 15:45). He is not only the Giver and Sender of the Spirit, but in resurrection He became the life-giving Spirit. Hence, 2 Corinthians 3:17 tells us that He is the Spirit.

The Alpha and Omega, the First and the Last, the Beginning and the End

In Revelation, the last book of the Bible, the Lord declared that He is the Alpha and Omega (22:13). Alpha and Omega are the first and last letters of the Greek alphabet. To say that Christ is the Alpha and Omega means that He is every letter in the alphabet. He is not only the first letter and the last, but He is every letter. Therefore, in Revelation 22:13 the Lord continued to declare that He is the First and the Last, and that He is the beginning and the end. This means that He is all-inclusive. He is all twenty-four letters of the Greek alphabet, and He is every word composed with this alphabet. Furthermore, He is every sentence composed with all the words, and, moreover, He is the entire composition composed with all the sentences. Eventually, the entire composition is just Christ. Christ is all-inclusive.

The Eternal Life

Such an all-inclusive Christ is the eternal life (1 John 2). He is the eternal life for us and to us that we may experience Him.

The Mystery of God

Colossians 2:2 tells us that Christ is the mystery of God. God is mysterious. God Himself is a mystery, and this mystery is fully revealed by Christ and in Christ. That Christ is God's mystery indicates that if we desire to know God, we must know Christ. Christ is the definition and explanation of God. Christ is also the expression of God. Everything concerning God is in Christ.

The Embodiment of the Triune God

Christ is the very embodiment of the Triune God. Colossians 2:9 tells us that in Christ dwells all the fullness of the Godhead bodily. All the fullness of the Godhead refers to the Trinity—the Father, the Son, and the Spirit. The divine Trinity is the fullness of the Godhead, and this fullness of the Godhead dwells in Christ. Therefore, Christ is the embodiment of the Triune God. The Father, the Son, and the Spirit are all embodied in Christ.

Christ, our Redeemer and our Savior, is all-inclusive. As such an all-inclusive One, He is the complete God. We need to spend much time to enter into the significance of all the foregoing details regarding Christ's Person, until we are fully saturated and immersed in these things. Then we shall realize that the Triune God—the Father, the Son, and the Spirit—is one God who is embodied in the Person of Christ. When we receive Christ, we receive the Triune God. When we enjoy Christ, we enjoy the Triune God. When we experience Him, we experience the Father, the Son, and the Spirit. How wonderful this is!

CHAPTER TWO

CHRIST—THE PERFECT MAN

Scripture Reading: Matt. 1:18, 20; Luke 1:35; John 1:14;
1 Tim. 3:16; Rom. 8:3; John 3:14; Num. 21:8-9; 2 Cor. 5:21;
1 Cor. 15:45b, 47b; Isa. 53:2-3; Col. 1:15; John 1:29; Gen. 3:15;
Heb. 2:14; John 12:31; Gen. 12:3; Gal. 3:14, 16; 2 Sam. 7:12-13;
Matt. 1:1; 16:18-19; 1:21; Luke 2:11; Matt. 16:16a; Col. 1:20;
Heb. 2:9; Eph. 2:14-15; John 12:24

THE COMPLETE GOD
AND THE PERFECT MAN

For us to experience Christ, we must receive a revelation
concerning His Person. We must see the two major aspects concerning the Person of Christ. The first aspect is that He is the
complete God, and the second aspect is that He is the perfect
man. Christ is both the complete God and the perfect man. In
brief, He is both God and man. We do have a wonderful Christ.
He is not only wonderful as the complete God, but He is also
wonderful as the perfect man.

THE PERFECT MAN

In this chapter we will see seventeen items concerning
Christ as the perfect man. If we do not have a clear vision con-
cerning Christ as these seventeen items, we cannot know
Christ in full.

Conceived of the Holy Spirit
in a Human Virgin

This perfect Man, Christ, was conceived of the Holy Spirit
in a human virgin (Matt. 1:18, 20; Luke 1:35). The conception of a person is the constitution of that person. Christ was

constituted of the Holy Spirit in a human virgin. As we saw
in the previous message, the Holy Spirit is the Triune God.
When we touch any One of the Three, the Father, the Son,
or the Spirit, we touch the Triune God. Both Matthew 1:18
and 20 and Luke 1:35 tell us that Christ was conceived of the
Holy Spirit. This means that the very Christ was conceived of
the Triune God. He was conceived of the Holy Spirit, yet in a
human virgin. The word Holy refers to the Spirit, indicating
the complete God, and the word human refers to mankind,
since a virgin is part of mankind. This means that Christ was
conceived of the complete God in humanity.

In the conception of Christ, there were two essences—the
essence of God and the essence of man. On one hand, Christ
was conceived of the Triune God. This involves the essence of
God. On the other hand, He was born of a human virgin. This
involves the essence of man. Hence, Christ is constituted of
the essence of God and the essence of man. Among mankind
there has been no other one like this. Only Christ was
conceived of God in humanity.

Born a God-man with the
Divine Nature and the Human Nature

Because Christ was constituted of God and man in His
conception, He was born a God-man. A person who is conceived
of certain elements will be born to be a composition of those
elements. Because Christ was conceived of God and man, He
was born a God-man. This means He is both God and man.
He is both the complete God and the perfect man.

In the four Gospels we can see in Christ the marvelous
and mysterious God. Yet, in the same Christ we can also see
an ordinary man. He is nothing less than God, and He is
nothing short of a genuine man. The life He lived was the life
of a man. He walked, He worked, He talked to people, and He
ate and drank as a man. While living as a man, He also lived
God. In His human life, God was expressed, yet while He was
expressing God, He was a genuine man. This is the reason
that when Christ was living on this earth, many people
watching Him would say, "Who is this man?" This man is not
simple. He is both God and man. In Him, the one Person, we

see both God and man. This is wonderful! Have you ever seen such a man? I have been a Christian for nearly sixty years. On one hand, I cannot deny that I have seen Christ because I have received a revelation concerning Him. But if you ask me about the color of His eyes or the length of His hair, I would tell you that I have never seen Him in this way. He is a wonderful Person. He is so real and genuine, yet no one can see Him. Nevertheless, we touch Him and enjoy Him daily. He is wonderful because He is both God and man.

God Incarnated in the Flesh

Christ was also God incarnated in the flesh. John 1:14 says that the Word, which was God (John 1:1), became flesh. Christ was God manifested in the flesh (1 Tim. 3:16). But there is a big contrast between God and the flesh. God is wonderful and excellent, but in the flesh there is nothing good (Rom. 7:18). Because the flesh is so troublesome, many times I have hated my flesh. Although there is nothing good in the flesh, Christ was God incarnated in the flesh.

In the Likeness of the Flesh of Sin

Christ was indeed God incarnated in the flesh, but He was only in the likeness of the flesh of sin (Rom. 8:3). When He was walking on this earth, He was in the same likeness as all mankind. In appearance, in likeness, He was the same as all human beings, who are flesh. But in reality, He was not the flesh. In Numbers 21:8-9 God told Moses to lift up a brass serpent. That brass serpent had the form of a serpent, but did not have the nature and poison of a serpent. In John 3:14 Jesus said, "As Moses lifted up the serpent in the wilderness, even so must the Son of Man be lifted up." He was to be lifted up on the cross as the brass serpent to condemn Satan, the old serpent, with his nature of sin. This is too mysterious. It is far beyond our understanding.

In His crucifixion, Christ was typified by a brass serpent. When He was crucified on the cross, in the eyes of God He was just like that serpent. He was a serpent in appearance, in form, but not in nature. Many Christians know that Christ is the Lamb of God, but very few know that Christ was also the brass serpent. We may appreciate the Lamb of God, but we may not like to hear that Christ was the brass serpent. But although John 1:29 says that Jesus is the Lamb of God, John 3:14 says that Christ was typified by the brass serpent. In the same Gospel we are told that Christ is the Lamb of God and that Christ is the brass serpent. He was the Lamb of God to take away our sin in order to solve our problem of sin, and He was the brass serpent to deal with the old serpent, Satan. We do have these two great problems—sin and Satan. As the Lamb of God, Christ took away our sin. As the brass serpent, Christ destroyed the old serpent (Heb. 2:14). We all must say, "Hallelujah! Our sin has been taken away and Satan has been destroyed!" For destroying Satan, Christ had the form of a serpent, that is, the likeness of the flesh of sin, and in this flesh He condemned Satan and destroyed him.

Made Sin for Us

Christ was made sin for us. You may say, "Please do not say this. Do not say that Christ was made sin." But Paul tells us in 2 Corinthians 5:21 that Christ was made sin for us by God. When Christ was hanging on the cross, He was sin in the eyes of God. On the cross, God made Christ sin for us. Christ not only bore our sins on the cross, but He was also made sin for us. He was made sin for us by becoming a man in the flesh. Every man in the flesh is sin. If you were to ask me, "Brother, what are you?" I would have to answer, "I am nothing but sin." What are we? We are nothing but sin. We are not only sinners, but we are sin. You may think that you are a kind and humble gentleman, but in reality, you are nothing but sin. We are not only sinners, but we are sin itself.

That Christ became flesh means that Christ became sin. He became sin for us in order to condemn sin. Romans 8:3 says, "God sending His own Son in the likeness of the flesh of sin and concerning sin, condemned sin in the flesh." When Christ was crucified on the cross, sin was condemned. When He was crucified on the cross as sin, sin was crucified. When He was crucified on the cross as a brass serpent, Satan was destroyed. By this we can see that Christ's being a man is not a simple matter.

The Last Adam and the Second Man

Christ was the last Adam and He is the second Man. There were only two Adams, the first Adam and the last Adam (1 Cor. 15:45). The first Adam was Adam our fore-father, and the last Adam was Christ. The last Adam is the conclusion of Adam. The last of anything is the end of that thing. So, the last Adam is the end of Adam. Christ became a man. As a man, He ended the Adamic race. Hallelujah, Adam is terminated in Christ!

Christ is also the second Man (1 Cor. 15:47). In the universe there are only two Adams and two men. The first Adam was Adam our forefather and the last Adam was Christ. The first man was Adam and the second Man was Christ. The last Adam indicates an ending, and the second Man indicates a new beginning. Christ's being the last Adam means that He terminated Adam. Christ's being the second Man indicates that He is a new beginning. We were all in Adam, and we were all terminated in Christ. Now we are in the second Man, and we are in the new beginning. Hallelujah, in Christ as the last Adam we have been terminated, and in Christ as the second Man we are in the new beginning! To be terminated is to be crucified; to be in the new beginning is to be in resurrection. We are in Christ as the last Adam, and we are also in Him as the second Man. In Him, on one hand, we have been terminated, and in Him, on the other hand, we have a new beginning.

A Man of Sorrows
and a Root out of Dry Ground

Isaiah 53:2-3 tells us that Christ was a Man of sorrows and that Christ was a root out of dry ground. Dry ground is earth in which there is no nourishment and no water. The Lord Jesus was born into a poor family. That carpenter's home in Nazareth was like the dry ground. In His human life there was nothing but suffering, so Isaiah gave Him the title "a Man of sorrows." This means Christ has tasted all the sufferings of the human life. As a man, He was a Man of sorrows.

The Firstborn of All Creation

Colossians 1:15 says that Christ is the Firstborn of all creation. This is wonderful! Since Christ became a man and a man is a creature, Christ surely became a creature. As God, He is the Creator. As man, He is one of the creatures. Many Christians today would not dare say that Christ is a creature. Yet, they recognize that Christ became a man. As Christ is a man, He is surely also a creature. He put on the blood, flesh, skin, and bones of man (Heb. 2:14; Luke 24:39). All of these are created things; hence, Christ is the Firstborn of all creation.

The Lamb of God

John 1:29 tells us that Christ is the Lamb of God. Again, as the Lamb Christ must be a creature. If He were not a creature, He would not have had blood to shed for sinners. Christ was offered to God as the Lamb mainly to shed His blood to redeem us from our sins (Eph. 1:7; 1 Pet. 1:18-19).

The Seed of Woman— the Bruiser of the Old Serpent

Christ was the seed of woman and the bruiser of the old serpent. Genesis 3:15 prophesied that the seed of woman would bruise the head of the serpent. This means that such a seed of woman would destroy Satan. Through death, Christ destroyed Satan (Heb. 2:14), and Satan, as the ruler of this world, was judged by Christ on the cross (John 12:31).

The Seed of Abraham— the Blessing to All the Nations

As a man, Christ is also the seed of Abraham (Gal. 3:16). This seed is the blessing to all the nations (Gen. 22:18; Gal. 3:14). In becoming a man, Christ became a blessing to all the peoples on this earth. This was prophesied in Genesis 22 and fulfilled in Galatians 3.

The Seed of David— the Builder of God's House and God's Kingdom

Christ is also the seed of David (Matt. 1:1; Rom. 1:3). As

the seed of David, He is the builder of God's house and of God's kingdom. Solomon, the son of David, built the temple and the kingdom of Israel (2 Sam. 7:12-13). Christ is the seed of David to build up the temple, the church, as the house of God and the kingdom of God (Matt. 16:18-19; 1 Tim. 3:15).

Jesus—Jehovah the Savior

As a man, this Christ is Jesus, which means "Jehovah the Savior" (Matt. 1:21; Luke 2:11). Jehovah is the Triune God, and He became Jesus. This means He became our Savior.

Christ—God's Anointed One

Christ is also the Christ (Matt. 16:16a), which means the anointed One. As God's Anointed, Christ's commission is to carry out God's purpose.

The Redeemer of All Created Things

Christ is the Redeemer of all created things. Colossians 1:20 says that not only man, but also all things in the heavens and on the earth have been reconciled through Christ. Furthermore, Hebrews 2:9 says that Christ died to taste death on behalf of everything. This is clearly typified by the redemption of Noah's ark, in which not only eight persons, but all other living things created by God were saved (Gen. 7:13-23).

The Peacemaker

Christ is the Peacemaker, and as the Peacemaker He is our peace (Eph. 2:14-15). He has made peace between us and God and among all the different peoples. The Jews could never be one with the Gentiles, and the Germans could never be one with the British. But Christ died on the cross to abolish all the differences between the peoples (Eph. 2:15; Col. 3:11). He made peace for all the different peoples so that we all can be one in Him. As a man, He is the Peacemaker.

The Grain of Wheat

Finally, as a man, Christ was a grain of wheat which brought forth many grains through death and resurrection. He told us in John 12:24 that He, as the grain of wheat, had to fall into the ground and die in order to produce many grains. We the believers are these many grains to be the members of His Body (1 Cor. 10:17). Therefore, the issue of Christ's being a man is the producing of His Body.

CHAPTER THREE

THE WORK OF CHRIST

(1)

Scripture Reading: Matt. 4:17; 16:18-19; Mark 1:1, 14; 4:3, 26; Luke 4:18-22a; 19:2-10; 10:30-37; John 1:18; 14:9; 5:30b; 6:38; 1:29; 2 Cor. 5:21; Rom. 8:3; Heb. 2:14; John 3:14; Num. 21:8-9; Rom. 6:6; 1 Cor. 15:45a; Col. 1:15, 20; Heb. 2:9; Eph. 2:14-15; John 12:24

In the previous two chapters we have covered a number of points concerning the Person of Christ. Beginning with this chapter we will go on to see a number of points concerning His work. We must spend adequate time to study and consider all these points. This will help us to enjoy Christ.

Today many Christians know Christ only in a superficial way. Although they would say that they love the Lord, if you were to ask them why they love Him they would have little to answer. But I hope that, after reading these chapters, we all could give many points as the reasons for which we love the Lord Jesus. We should be able to give at least fifteen points concerning Him as the complete God and at least seventeen points concerning Him as the perfect man. If possible, we should develop every point in detail. Then we should be able to go on and speak concerning all that He has done for us, how He ministered on this earth for us, entered into death for us, rose from the dead for us, and ascended to the heavens for us. He has done so much for us, and He is still doing so much in the heavens for us. This is why we love Him. We love Him because of what He is and because of what He has done for us. I hope that from now on every day while we are contacting, enjoying, and experiencing the Lord, we would experience Him in all these items.

When we enjoy a feast, we know all the courses we are about to eat, and we enjoy the feast dish by dish. However, many of us enjoy the Lord Jesus without an adequate knowledge concerning Him as the complete God and the perfect man. Furthermore, we often enjoy Him without knowing adequately how much He has done for us. We know that He worked and ministered on the earth, but we do not know specifically what He did. We know that He died on the cross, but we do not realize the crucial points concerning His death. We know that He rose from the dead, but we do not know what His resurrection has accomplished. We know that He ascended, but we do not know how much He has accomplished through His ascension. Since we are limited in knowing Christ, our experience of Him is also quite restricted. This is why there is the need for a book such as this, that we might see who Christ is and what He has done for us, that we might enjoy Him and experience Him in full.

The New Testament tells us repeatedly that we need to have a full knowledge of Christ and His work (Eph. 1:17-23; 4:13; Col. 2:2). In the Bible Christ is revealed not in a simple way but in a very detailed way. It is not adequate simply to know that Christ is God. You must know the details of Christ being God, how He is the self-existing and ever-existing God, how He is the universal "To Be," how He is the Triune God Jehovah, how He is the Creator, and so forth. You must dive into and digest all these items as well as all the points concerning Christ's work. Then while you are studying all these points, you will appreciate Him and enjoy Him. Such a study will usher you into the full enjoyment of Christ.

RECEIVING THE REVELATION
CONCERNING THE WORK OF CHRIST

After receiving the revelation concerning the Person of Christ, we need to receive a revelation concerning His work. The work of Christ is composed of four major items: His ministry on earth, His crucifixion, His resurrection, and His ascension. In this chapter we will consider the first two items of Christ's work, and in the following chapter we will consider the last two items.

HIS MINISTRY ON EARTH

The first item of Christ's work is His ministry on the earth. As a man the Lord Jesus lived on this earth for thirty-three and a half years, but it was not until the last three and a half years that He came out to minister. In His ministry He did many things for God, and He did many things for man. The New Testament contains four Gospels to tell us what He did in His ministry on the earth. If we do not spend time and pay full attention to find out the different aspects of Christ's ministry portrayed in each of the four Gospels, we will have only a general knowledge of His ministry on the earth. We might consider that the four Gospels are nearly the same, with only slight differences in presentation; but this is absolutely not the case.

In Matthew—Preaching the Gospel of the Kingdom and Bringing In the Kingdom of the Heavens

In Matthew we see that Christ came out to preach a particular gospel, the gospel of the kingdom (Matt. 4:17). This is different from the gospel of grace and from the gospel of forgiveness. It is the gospel of the kingdom, and it brings people into the kingdom of the heavens. Matthew tells us that this Christ brought in the kingdom of the heavens and that He even gave the keys of the kingdom of the heavens to one of His disciples, Peter (Matt. 16:18-19). Today few Christians have an adequate knowledge concerning the kingdom of the heavens, concerning the keys of the kingdom of the heavens, and concerning what it means to bring the kingdom of the heavens to people or to bring people into the kingdom of the heavens.

In Mark—Preaching the Gospel of God and Sowing the Seed of the Kingdom of God

Following Matthew's Gospel, Mark tells us that this Christ preached the gospel of God (Mark 1:1, 14). We might consider that the gospel of the kingdom and the gospel of God are just one gospel. However, just as we see a different view of one person from different angles, we also see different aspects of this wonderful gospel in each of the four Gospels. Viewing the gospel from one side, we see in Matthew the gospel of the kingdom which brings sinners into a heavenly kingdom. From another side, we see in Mark the gospel of God which brings sinners into God. Mark presents Christ as the One who brings us into God, whereas Matthew presents Christ as the One who brings us into the kingdom of the heavens. Today, this same Christ is still preaching the gospel of God to bring us into God, and He is still preaching the gospel of the kingdom to bring us into the kingdom of the heavens. I hope that we all may have at least some experience and enjoyment of Christ in this way. Then we will say, "Oh Lord, You are the One who brings me into God, and You are the One who brings me into the kingdom of the heavens. I enjoy You not only as my Redeemer and my Savior but as the One who brings me into God and into the kingdom of the heavens."

In Matthew Christ brought in the kingdom of the heavens, and in Mark He sowed Himself as the seed of the kingdom (Mark 4:1-20). We may use the planting of a carnation seed as an illustration. First, we have only the carnation seed. Then we sow the seed of the carnation into a field, and the seed grows, bringing forth the blossom of the carnation. Soon in that field we will see a garden full of carnation blossoms. That is the kingdom of carnation. What is the kingdom of God? The kingdom of God is just God blossoming. Jesus came to sow Himself as the seed of God into man's heart. Man's heart is the field, and Jesus as the seed of God is growing in our heart. When this seed in our heart blossoms, it becomes a garden of God. This garden is the kingdom of God, a garden with God blossoming. This garden today is the church. Today in Japan there is such a little garden, a garden of God with God blossoming. The proper church life is the kingdom of God, which is God blossoming from within so many believers.

In Luke—Proclaiming the Jubilee and Carrying Out His Dynamic Salvation by the Virtue of His Highest Standard of Morality

In the Gospel of Luke, Christ is presented as the One who proclaimed the jubilee (Luke 4:18-22). The jubilee is a release.

In the Old Testament jubilee any man who had sold his land or had sold himself into slavery would be released from captivity and brought back to his own inheritance (Lev. 25:8-17). The background of the Lord's New Testament jubilee is that all men are captives. Why is everyone so busy? Because they all are captives. The students are captives, and the professors are also captives. Even the world rulers are captives. All of fallen mankind has been carried away and is held captive by Satan. Therefore, all have lost their inheritance, which is God Himself. Although God is man's portion and man's inheritance, all of fallen mankind has lost God. They all have become captives; they all have become poor. According to Luke's Gospel, Jesus came to proclaim the jubilee, to announce the release of the captives, to set them all free from Satan, and to bring them all back to God.

Luke chapter fifteen tells the story of the prodigal son. He was one who lost all the inheritance in his father's house. But one day he was brought back. That was his being set free. He was brought back to his father's house to enjoy the riches of the father's house. That was his being brought back to his inheritance. Before we were saved we were all captives, carried away from God by many sinful things and even by things that may be considered good. But one day the Lord Jesus brought us back. He set us free from our captivity and brought us back to God. Now we enjoy our inheritance. Now we are in the enjoyment of the jubilee. This was the work of Christ, to announce the jubilee and to carry out the jubilee among us.

After Mark presents Christ coming to preach the gospel of God and to sow the seed of the kingdom of God, Luke presents the same Christ coming to proclaim the jubilee, to set the captives free, and to bring them all back to God as their inheritance. This is Christ's dynamic salvation which is by the virtue of His highest standard of morality.

This dynamic salvation is seen in Luke chapter nineteen in the case of Zaccheus. Zaccheus was a sinful tax collector, robbing people by means of extortion. He was an infamous tax collector, rejected and condemned by his community. One day he heard that Jesus was coming. But he was a short man, and a large crowd was gathered to see Jesus. So in order to see Jesus, he climbed a sycamore tree. As Jesus came to the place where he was, He looked up and called him by name, "Zaccheus, hurry and come down; for today I must stay in your house" (v. 5). Although Zaccheus was rejected by everyone, this Jesus nevertheless called him by name and told him that He was coming to visit his family. Simply by Jesus visiting the house of Zaccheus, there was a great change in the life of Zaccheus. He immediately told the Lord Jesus that he would give half of his wealth to the poor, and that whatever he had taken from anyone by false accusations, he would restore four times as much (v. 8). Following this, the Lord Jesus said, "Today salvation has come to this house." This is the Lord's dynamic salvation.

The salvation we have received is not a weak salvation but a powerful salvation, even a dynamic salvation. This dynamic salvation is by virtue of the highest standard of the Lord's morality, which is composed of His divine attributes mingled with His human virtues. The virtues of Confucius cannot compare with those of Jesus. To compare the virtues of Confucius with those of Jesus is like comparing gold and brass. The standard of Jesus' morality is much higher than that of Confucius. The morality of Confucius was merely human, but the morality of Jesus is heavenly and divinely human. The Lord's morality was produced by the divine attributes in the human virtues, and it was a morality of the highest standard. This highest morality is the virtue of Christ's dynamic salvation.

In John—
Living God and Doing the Father's Will

John's Gospel reveals that Christ lived God and did the Father's will. He lived a life which was God Himself. No one has ever seen God, but Christ as the Son of God expressed Him (John 1:18). Christ lived a life manifesting God the Father and making Him known (John 14:9). At the same time He did the Father's will (John 5:30b; 6:38). He did not do His own work or accomplish His own intention but did the Father's will. When we see this, we will enjoy Christ and experience Him as the One who lives God and who does the will of God. This will enable us also to live God and to do the will of God. The more we enjoy Christ and experience Him, the more we will live God, express God, and do God's will.

If you put together all the aspects of Christ's work in the four Gospels you will see the ministry He carried out on this earth. I hope that you will take the time to study Matthew, Mark, Luke, and John with all the footnotes of the Recovery Version and the Life-study Messages on the four Gospels. If you do this, you will experience Christ and enjoy Him much more. Then in Japan there will be a garden of God to grow God and express Him. The Lord today needs a number of blossoming Christians, those who know Him, experience Him, and enjoy Him.

HIS CRUCIFIXION

The second category of Christ's work is His crucifixion. In man's eyes, to die is not a work; but concerning Christ, His dying was a great work, a great accomplishment. While He was on the cross He was working, and when He entered Hades He was also working. Although it was unseen to human eyes, Satan with all the evil spirits knew that while Christ was dying on the cross, He was truly doing a great work. His working on the cross eventually became a battle, with God "stripping off the rulers and the authorities... triumphing over them" (Col. 2:15). While Christ was dying on the cross, Satan was there fighting. Whenever the police go to arrest a robber, there is always a struggle and a fight. The death of Christ on the cross was the arrest of Satan. In Genesis 3, God promised that Christ would bruise the head of the serpent (Gen. 3:15), and when Christ died on the cross, He destroyed the Devil (Heb. 2:14). Now let us consider all the accomplishments of Christ's crucifixion.

To Take Away Sin

The first accomplishment of Christ's crucifixion was that He took away sin by being killed as the Lamb of God (John 1:29). John 1:29 says, "Behold, the Lamb of God who takes away the sin of the world!" Do you realize how heavy is the load of the sin of the world? The load of sin is like a great mountain, but Christ's death as the Lamb of God removed this mountain of sin. This was a great work accomplished by Christ in His death. The word sin in John 1:29 denotes the aggregate, the totality, of sin and of sins. In the Bible sin in the singular denotes our inward sinful nature (2 Cor. 5:21; Heb. 9:26), whereas sins in the plural number denotes our outward sinful deeds (1 Pet. 3:18; 1 Cor. 15:3; Heb. 9:28). Within man there is a sinful nature called sin, and outwardly there are many sinful activities called sins. The word sin in John 1:29 denotes the aggregate, the totality, of sin within and sins without. This totality of sin is a great load. Yet Christ took the load away. He removed this high mountain by being the Lamb of God dying on the cross. He was killed on the cross as the Lamb of God to be the greatest offering, the sin offering for sin and the trespass offering for sins. As the Lamb of God He was killed as the sin offering and as the trespass offering to remove the totality of sin and of sins from the world. Since Christ has done such a marvelous work, we must announce such a glad tiding, that sin has been removed.

To Cause Sin to Be Condemned

The second accomplishment of Christ's crucifixion is that sin in the flesh was condemned by God through Christ who was made sin on the cross for the believers (2 Cor. 5:21; Rom. 8:3). To take away sin is one thing, but to be made sin is another. First, Christ took away sin, and, second, Christ was made sin. First, Christ came as the Lamb of God to take away the load of sin from fallen man. But this fallen man is still sin. Fallen man not only carries a load of sin, but the fallen man himself is sin. Therefore Christ as the Lamb of God first took away the load of sin; but to deal with the fallen man himself Christ had to do a further work. This further work was for Christ to be made sin (2 Cor. 5:21).

Fallen man is sin because fallen man is flesh (Rom. 3:20). Therefore, in order to condemn sin Christ became flesh (John 1:14). But when Christ became flesh, He came only in the likeness of the flesh of sin (Rom. 8:3), just as the brass serpent was only in the form of the serpent (John 3:14). Christ became flesh in the likeness of the flesh of sin. He Himself was not the flesh of sin, but He was in the likeness, the form, of the flesh of sin. It was in this likeness of the flesh of sin that He was made sin. He was not a serpent in nature, in poison, but only in form. He had no sin (Heb. 4:15). Second Corinthians 5:21 even says that He knew no sin. He was only in the form of the sinful flesh. While He was in the form, the likeness, of the sinful flesh, He was made sin and died in this flesh. By His dying in the flesh, sin was condemned by God (Rom. 8:3). This means that He terminated both sin and the flesh. Sin was condemned through Christ who was made sin on the cross for the believers.

To Destroy Satan

The third accomplishment of Christ's crucifixion was that He destroyed Satan, the old serpent, by being judged by God as the brass serpent (Heb. 2:14; John 3:14; Num. 21:8-9). When Christ was crucified on the cross, God saw Him first as the Lamb, second, as the flesh which was sin, and, third, as a brass serpent. As the Lamb He took away sin, as the flesh He caused sin to be condemned by God, and as the brass serpent He destroyed the old serpent, Satan.

To Deal with the Old Man

The fourth accomplishment of Christ's crucifixion was that He dealt with the old man by being crucified as the last Adam (Rom. 6:6; 1 Cor. 15:45a). We must realize that a fallen person is not so simple. Fallen man is not only carrying a load of sin, but he himself also is sin. Furthermore, within him there is the old serpent, Satan, and he also has the old man, the old self. Man has a problem with sin, the flesh, Satan, and the old man. As the Lamb of God Christ took away the load of sin; through His being in the likeness of the flesh of sin, sin was condemned; as the brass serpent Christ destroyed the old serpent, Satan; and through Him as the last Adam, the old man was crucified.

To Deal with the Old Creation

The fifth accomplishment of Christ's crucifixion was that He dealt with the old creation by being terminated as the Firstborn of all creation (Col. 1:15), and He redeemed all the creation by tasting death for everything (Col. 1:20; Heb.2:9). Christ is the first item of the creatures, the Firstborn of all creation. As such a One He dealt with the old creation. His crucifixion was a termination of the old creation, and He redeemed all the creation by tasting death for everything. Christ was qualified for this accomplishment because He was one of the creatures, the Firstborn of God's creation. Because He was a creature, His crucifixion was the termination of all the old creation. By such a work He redeemed all the created things, because through His death He tasted death for everything, not only for every person, but also for every thing.

To Make Peace among All Peoples

According to Ephesians 2:14-15, Christ's death was to make peace among all peoples. This is the sixth accomplishment of Christ's crucifixion. Christ was crucified as the Peacemaker to make peace among all peoples by abolishing all the ordinances, the differences, among them. Ephesians 2:14-15 say, "For He Himself is our peace, who has made both one, and has broken down the middle wall of partition, the enmity, having abolished in His flesh the law of the commandments in ordinances, that He might create the two in Himself into one new man, making peace." In these verses, Christ is both our peace and the Peacemaker. Because of the fall, the entire human race has been divided into many nations. No two nations are able to be one, especially the Jewish nation and the Gentile nations, because of many differences, many ordinances. The ordinances are the habits, the customs, the ways of living, and the ways of religion among people.

Through His death on the cross, Christ abolished all the differences among the peoples of the earth. By making peace He brought the different nations, the different peoples, together into oneness. Today we can see many different peoples from different nations as brothers in the church. This peacemaking is to produce the Body of Christ which is the new man. Christ abolished all the differences, the ordinances among the different peoples, in order to create one new man out of so many believers from different nations. Today in the testimony of the local churches we see such a reality. For example, in the United States we recently had a meeting of approximately one thousand people, with representatives from more than thirty nationalities. In the church, although there are people of many different races, all are brothers, all are members, all are components of this one new man! Hallelujah! Who did this? Christ did this on the cross, by dying in the flesh to abolish all the ordinances. Christ died as such a Peacemaker.

To Bring Forth Many Grains

The seventh accomplishment of Christ's crucifixion was to bring forth many grains. He did this by being put to death as a grain of wheat (John 12:24). The first six items—to take away sin, to have sin condemned, to destroy Satan, to have the old man crucified, to terminate the old creation, and to abolish all the ordinances between different peoples—are all on the negative side. But there is also a positive side, the bringing forth of His believers as many grains. Christ accomplished this by being put to death as a grain of wheat. On the one hand, a grain of wheat sown into the earth dies. But, on the other hand, while the grain is dying, it is growing. While the grain is dying in its outward shell, it is growing in its inner life. By its dying and growing, it sprouts; something tender, green, and living rises up to bring forth many grains. While Christ was dying on the cross, He was working, He was growing, and He was bringing forth many grains. Hallelujah! Now, we are the many grains to form one loaf, one Body (1 Cor. 10:17).

These are the seven main items of the work Christ has accomplished by His death on the cross. To do this sevenfold work He has a sevenfold qualification: He is the Lamb of God, He is a man in the likeness of the flesh of sin, He is the brass serpent, He is the last Adam, He is the Firstborn of all creation, He is the Peacemaker, and He is the grain of wheat.

We all must see that when our Redeemer was dying on the cross, He was dying there as these seven items. He died as the Lamb of God, as a man in the likeness of the flesh of sin, as a brass serpent, as the last Adam, as the Firstborn of all creation, as the Peacemaker, and as the grain of wheat. By this sevenfold qualification He accomplished seven things: He took away sin, He caused sin to be condemned in the flesh, He destroyed the old serpent, He had the old man crucified, He terminated and redeemed the old creation, He abolished all the differences between the nations, and He produced many grains. Now the new man, the Body of Christ, is here. All this has been accomplished by His sevenfold work on the cross.

CHAPTER FOUR

THE WORK OF CHRIST

(2)

Scripture Reading: Acts 3:15; 5:30-31; Rom. 4:25; Acts 13:33; Rom. 8:29; John 12:24; 1 Pet. 1:3; John 12:28; 13:31-32; 17:1; Luke 24:26; 1 Cor. 15:45b; John 20:22; Acts 2:36; Eph. 1:22, 10; Acts 2:33; 1 Cor. 12:13; Heb. 7:22; 8:6; 9:15-17; 4:15; 7:26; Rev. 1:13; 2:1; 1:5; 5:5-6

In the three foregoing chapters we pointed out that in order to experience Christ, we first need to receive revelation concerning the Person and work of Christ. In the last chapter we covered what Christ accomplished in His life on earth and in His death. We pointed out that there are eight main points concerning His work on the earth, two points in each of the four Gospels. Then we covered seven main things which the Lord accomplished through His death. Thus, in the previous chapters we have seen fifteen items of Christ's work. In this chapter we shall consider another fifteen items accomplished by Christ, seven items in His resurrection and eight in His ascension.

Many Christians today do not have an accurate and adequate view concerning Christ's resurrection and ascension. Because of this lack, their experience of Christ is inadequate. Believers today often speak about Christ's death, but they do not speak as much about His resurrection and ascension. Many Christians see very little concerning Christ's ascension. They only know that Christ went to the heavens and is waiting there until the time of His return. However, the New Testament tells us very much about what Christ is doing now in the heavens. In one sense, He is doing more in the heavens than He did on the earth. Those who read the four Gospels can easily see that while Jesus was on the earth, He did many things such as working miracles and preaching the gospel. But when they read the Acts, the Epistles, and Revelation, few realize what Christ is doing now in the heavens. Not only is Christ doing many things in the heavens today, but He also accomplished many things before He ascended. We need to be impressed with all the crucial and wonderful things Christ has done in His resurrection and ascension.

HIS RESURRECTION

To Prove That God Has Accepted
His All-inclusive Redemptive Work

The resurrection of Christ was a great proof that God had accepted His all-inclusive redemptive work (Acts 3:15). After Christ had finished His work on earth, He died on the cross to accomplish God's redemption. His redemptive work was exceedingly great. However, in the eyes of the Jews, Christ was rejected by God. They would not believe that God was one with Christ, that God would accept what Christ had done. Their thought was that Christ had blasphemed God and was against God (Matt. 26:65). So they rejected Him by crucifying Him and putting Him into a tomb. The Jews thought that to put Christ into the tomb was to do a marvelous work for God. But, to their great surprise, God raised Him up. God did this in order to tell the Jews that He accepted what they rejected. God seemed to be saying, "You Jews should know that although you rejected Christ, put Him to death, and even put Him into a tomb, I, the very God whom you serve, raised this Man out of death." This is also confirmed by the word in Acts 2:23-24. Such a resurrection was a great and strong proof that God accepted, sealed, and vindicated all that Christ had done. The resurrection of Christ proved that God was very happy with all that Christ had done.

To Vindicate His Great Success
in All His Achievements

Christ's resurrection was a strong vindication of His great

success in all His achievements (Acts 5:30-31). In history there have been many great men. One of them was Alexander the Great, who lived about three hundred years before Christ. He conquered many countries while he was still under thirty-five years of age. Alexander came from Macedonia, the northern part of Greece. He built up and trained a strong army, and conquered Greece, Persia, and Egypt. But suddenly, at the age of thirty-three, he died. His death was a sign of his failure.

When the Jews put Christ to death, they thought that He was altogether defeated, and that His death was a sign of His failure. But after three days Christ came out of the tomb. So Christ's resurrection was a strong vindication of His great success. Many men have accomplished great things, but their success ended with their death. But although Jesus was put to death, God raised Him up. This raising up of Christ by God was a vindication of His great success. In human history there has never been another person as successful as Christ. His resurrection carried out His success, and His success is still continuing on the earth today. Confucius died, Mohammed died, and Socrates died. Many great men died and were buried. In human history, there has been only one exception. Only this One came out of the tomb and is still working today. He is moving, He is acting, and He is motivating all His people on the earth. He has obtained a great success, and this success was sealed by His resurrection.

To Evidence That God Has Justified the Believers

Christ's resurrection was also the evidence that God has justified us (Rom. 4:25). Because He died on the cross for our sins, God has to forgive us. But if Christ had never been raised from the dead, how could we know that God has forgiven us, that He was satisfied by Christ's death? Christ's resurrection from the dead was the evidence that God was satisfied by His death. Because God was content with Christ's death, God released Him from death.

To illustrate this point, let us suppose that a brother owes a certain rich man ten million dollars. The rich man holds a note for that loan which states clearly that the brother owes him ten million dollars. Now, let us suppose that I have the ability to pay his debt, and that I pay ten million dollars to the rich man. However, although he accepts my payment, the rich man will not give me a receipt. Without a receipt as evidence that I have repaid the loan, the brother has no way to prove that the rich man has been satisfied by my payment. But if the rich man gives me a receipt, I now can tell the brother the good news that I have paid his debt. I have the receipt as evidence that the rich man has released him from obligation because he has been satisfied by my payment.

In the same way, we know that God was satisfied by Christ's payment because God raised Him from the dead. Romans 4:25 says, "Who was delivered because of our offenses, and was raised because of our justification." The first part of this verse indicates that Christ died on the cross for our sins, and the second part tells us that because God was satisfied with Christ's death for our sins, He released Christ from death. Christ's coming out of death was a great proof that God was satisfied with His death for us. This resurrected Christ is the "receipt" of His full payment for our debt, issued by God to us, proving that all our sins have been forgiven and that God has justified us.

To Be Born as the Firstborn Son of God

The New Testament reveals that in Christ's resurrection, He was born as the firstborn Son of God. Acts 13:33 says, "God has fully fulfilled this promise to us their children in raising up Jesus, as it is also written in the second psalm, You are My Son; today I have begotten You." Furthermore, Romans 8:29 refers to Christ as God's Son, the Firstborn among many brothers. From these two verses we can see that on the day of resurrection, Jesus was begotten by God to be the firstborn Son of God.

Of course, Christ's incarnation was also a birth, but that birth made Him the Son of Man. Christ did not become the Son of God through incarnation. In eternity past, before His incarnation and before His resurrection, Christ was already the Son of God. The Bible reveals that Christ, the Son of

God, is eternal. God is triune—the Father, the Son, and the Spirit—and all Three are eternal. God the Father is eternal (Isa. 9:6), God the Son is eternal (Heb. 7:3), and God the Spirit is eternal (Heb. 9:14). To be eternal means to have no beginning and no ending. Students of the Bible sometimes use a circle to signify eternity. A circle has no beginning and no ending, and it is difficult to tell whether one point on a circle comes before or after another point. In the same way, the Father, the Son, and the Spirit are all eternal, having no beginning nor ending. Hebrews 7:3 tells us that the Son of God is eternal, having neither beginning of days nor end of life. The revelation in the Bible is not that the Father existed before the Son, that the Son came into being after the Father, or that the Spirit came after the Son. Rather, the Bible says that all Three are eternal.

The Son of God is eternal, yet this eternal Son of God was born as the Son of Man about two thousand years ago. In His incarnation He was born of Mary, and by that birth He became the Son of Man. Therefore, His incarnation is His first birth. But the Bible also tells us that Christ had a second birth. In His first birth Christ was born as the Son of Man, and in His second birth He was born as the firstborn Son of God. On the one hand, John 3:16 says, "For God so loved the world that He gave His only begotten Son." This verse indicates that Christ was God's only Son. On the other hand, Romans 8:29 says, "...that He should be the Firstborn among many brothers." Have you ever considered that Christ is the Son of God in two ways? In the first way He was God's only begotten Son, and in the second way He is the firstborn Son among many sons. Romans 8:29 says that the believers are to be conformed, not to the image of the only begotten Son, but to the image of God's firstborn Son.

At this point we need to ask ourselves what the difference is between the only begotten Son and the firstborn Son. Our first response may be to say that the only begotten Son had no brothers, but the firstborn Son has many brothers. Although this is true, we still need to ask what the difference is in the Son of God Himself. The difference between the only begotten Son of God in eternity past and the firstborn Son of God in resurrection is that in eternity past, before His incarnation, He possessed only divinity without humanity. But through the process of incarnation, He put on humanity. He passed through human living, entered into death, and came out in resurrection. In resurrection He still remained the Son of God according to His divinity, but there was something more; He also possessed the humanity He obtained through incarnation. The humanity He put on in incarnation was also brought into resurrection to share in the sonship. This is why Acts 13:33 says that on the day of resurrection, Christ was begotten of God to be God's Son. It means that resurrection "sonized" His humanity, made it also the Son of God. According to Acts 13:33, Christ's resurrection was a birth, making Him not only God's only begotten Son with divinity, but also God's firstborn Son with both divinity and humanity.

Today Christ is the Son of God in two respects: He is God's only begotten Son and He is also God's firstborn Son. However, if He were only God's only begotten Son, He could not have any brothers. To have us as His brothers, He must possess humanity; but as God's only begotten Son in eternity past, He possessed only divinity, not humanity. Nevertheless, in His incarnation Christ put on humanity, and through resurrection He brought this humanity into sonship. In this way He became God's firstborn Son with both divinity and humanity. Then, as the life-giving Spirit, He entered into us to make us also sons of God. Now we are the many sons of God being conformed to the image, not of God's only begotten Son, but of His firstborn Son. Therefore, as God's firstborn Son, Christ has many brothers. We all need to see that being born as the firstborn Son of God was a great work which Christ accomplished through His resurrection. Although it is clearly taught in the Bible, many Christians have never seen this matter.

On the day of His resurrection Christ was begotten by God in His humanity. He became the firstborn Son of God in order to produce many sons of God. We need to realize that the date of our regeneration was the date of Christ's resurrection. When Christ was resurrected from among the dead, we, all the believers, were resurrected with Him (1 Pet. 1:3). Through His resurrection He was born to be God's firstborn Son, and at the same time all His believers were born to be the many sons of God. On the day of Christ's resurrection, all God's chosen people were resurrected and were born to be God's many sons. Now God has many sons with both divinity and humanity. But among these many sons, only the Firstborn is His only begotten Son. This only begotten Son of God, in His resurrected humanity, is also the firstborn Son of God. As the firstborn Son of God, He has both divinity and humanity, and we His believers as God's many sons also possess both the human nature and the divine nature (2 Pet. 1:4). Now day by day we are being conformed to the image of God's firstborn Son (Rom. 8:29).

To Release His Divine Life for His Propagation

In His resurrection Christ also released His divine life for His propagation (John 12:24; 1 Pet. 1:3). When the Lord Jesus died as the grain of wheat, His inner divine life rose up to grow. In His resurrection this life was released to produce many grains as His multiplication. This multiplication is His propagation. The one grain was propagated into many grains. Christ accomplished this great work in His resurrection.

To Be Glorified That God May Be Glorified in Him

Furthermore, Christ's resurrection was His glorification that God might be glorified in Him (John 12:28; 13:31-32; 17:1; Luke 24:26). A carnation flower is an illustration of this. When a carnation seed is sown, in a sense the carnation blossom is concealed within the seed. But when the plant blossoms, the glory of the carnation flower is manifested. This blossoming is the glorification of the carnation. Similarly, when Christ became a man, God's divine life was concealed in His human shell. When Christ's death broke His human shell, His divine life was released. This releasing of the divine life was the glorification of Christ. At the same time it was also the glorification of the concealed God. Luke

24:26 says, "Was it not necessary for the Christ to suffer these things and to enter into His glory?" This word refers to His resurrection (1 Cor. 15:43a; Acts 3:13a, 15a). Therefore, this verse tells us that through His resurrection Christ entered into glory. Before He ascended to the heavens, Christ had already entered into glory. Christ was glorified in His resurrection, and in His glorification God was also glorified.

To Become the Life-giving Spirit That He May Enter into His Believers

In His resurrection Christ became the life-giving Spirit that He may enter into His believers (1 Cor. 15:45b; John 20:22). While He was in the flesh, He was only able to be among the believers. He had no way to enter into Peter, John, or any of the other disciples. But in resurrection Christ became the life-giving Spirit, and on the day of resurrection He came back to the disciples and breathed Himself as the Spirit into them. Becoming the life-giving Spirit to enter into the believers was another great work of Christ in resurrection.

HIS ASCENSION

Christ accomplished a great deal in His death, in His resurrection, and in His ascension. However, His work in His ascension has not yet been completed, but will continue until He comes back.

To Be Made Lord

Christ's ascension made Him the Lord (Acts 2:36a). Just as Christ is both God's only begotten Son from eternity past and God's firstborn Son in resurrection, so Christ being the Lord is also in two aspects. From eternity past, Christ is the Lord because He is the very God. But this Christ who is the very God one day put on humanity through incarnation. Then, as we have seen, this humanity was sonized through Christ's resurrection. It was then in Christ's ascension as a man that God made Him the Lord, not only in His divinity but also in His humanity. Now the One who is the Lord of the entire universe is not only God, but also a man, the God-man.

To Be Made Christ

Christ's ascension made Him the Christ of God (Acts 2:36b). Actually, He was the Christ already before His ascension (Matt. 16:16). He was even called Christ from His birth (Matt. 1:16). That was for Him to accomplish the first part of God's economy for the accomplishment of God's redemption and the release of the divine life by His earthly ministry. In His ascension He was officially inaugurated into the position of God's Christ, God's appointed One, to carry out the second part of God's economy for the producing and the building up of the church by His heavenly ministry. The title Lord refers to His lordship in possessing all the universe. The title Christ refers to His being made the One who carries out God's eternal purpose.

To Be Made Head over All Things to the Church That All Things May Be Headed Up in Him

Christ's ascension made Him Head over all things to the church (Eph. 1:22). In ascension Christ was made the Head over all things to the church and for the church. This means that whatever He is as the Head over all things is transmitted to the church for the church's participation in His attainment that all things may be headed up in Him (Eph. 1:10). He is the Head over all things, and He is also the focus, the center, of all things. All things will be headed up in Him through the church.

Satan's fall and the fall of man made the universe a place of confusion and disorder. But Christ's ascension made Him the Head over all things to the church to bring everything in the universe back into good order. Therefore, all things will one day be headed up in Christ. This will be in the new heavens and the new earth through the New Jerusalem, which is the ultimate consummation of the church.

To Baptize His Body in the Spirit

In His ascension Christ baptized all His believers into one Body in the Holy Spirit (Acts 2:33; 1 Cor. 12:13). In His death He redeemed all His believers, in His resurrection He caused all His believers to be regenerated, and in His ascension He baptized all His believers into one Body in the Holy Spirit. By these three steps of death, resurrection, and ascension, to redeem the believers, to cause them to be regenerated, and to baptize them, He produced a Body. He completed this producing of His Body by His ascension. This was a great work accomplished by Christ in His ascension.

To Be the Heavenly Minister

In His ascension, Christ also became the heavenly Minister (Heb. 8:1). As the Minister of the true (heavenly) tabernacle, He has obtained in His ascension a more excellent ministry (Heb. 8:6) to minister heaven, which is not only a place but a condition of life, into us that we may have the heavenly life and power to live a heavenly life on earth, as He did while He was here, to fulfill our heavenly calling (Heb. 3:1).

To Be the Mediator of a Better Covenant

In His death Christ made the better covenant for us with God. In ascension He became the Mediator, the Surety, of the better covenant made by Him through His death (Heb. 8:6; 9:15-17; 7:22). As the Mediator, He is the Executor in His heavenly ministry of the new covenant which became the new testament which He bequeathed to us by His death with all the riches of the new testament. As the Surety He is not only the pledge but also the Guarantor to guarantee all the blessings of the new testament bequeathed to us by His death.

In ascension Christ became the Executor of the new testament (9:15-17). The word testament means a will. In this will many blessings have been bequeathed to the believers. Every will requires someone to execute it, to carry it out. In His ascension Christ became such an Executor.

To Be the High Priest to Care for His Believers and to Dress the Lampstands—the Churches

In His ascension Christ is the High Priest to care for all the believers and to care for the lampstands—the churches (Heb. 4:15; 7:26; Rev. 1:13; 2:1). In the Old Testament type the priest cared for the lampstand by dressing it that the lampstand might shine brightly. Likewise, today in His ascension, Christ as our High Priest cares for His believers and cares for the churches as the lampstands.

To Be the Administrator of the Divine Government over the Universe

Finally, Christ's ascension made Him the Administrator of the divine government over the universe (Rev. 1:5; 5:5-6). This fact is fully revealed in the book of Revelation. In Revelation 1:5, Christ is called "the Ruler of the kings of the earth." Today the One who governs the entire world, the Administrator of the entire universe, is not any king, any president, or any world organization. The head Ruler of God's government over the universe is Christ. He is the King of kings and the Lord of lords, and He administrates the entire universe for the purpose of fulfilling God's eternal plan. All the world situation is under His rule, not under the control of any nation. Jesus Christ is the Administrator of today's universe.

Our experience confirms the fact that Christ is ruling over the world situation in order to fulfill God's purpose. I was born and raised in China. I had no thought of coming to America. But about thirty-five years ago the Lord managed the world situation in such a way that many of us in the churches were forced to leave mainland China and to go to Taiwan. Then later the Lord arranged the situation again, causing us to leave Taiwan and to go to America. In this way the Lord's recovery was brought into the English language. If we had never come from China to America, the Lord's recovery would have been concealed in the Chinese language. Today the English language is spoken worldwide. After the Lord's recovery entered into the English language, it was brought to six continents. It was Jesus Christ as the Administrator of the universe who did this. Hallelujah!

Today in His ascension Christ is managing and administrating the entire universe. He will continue to do this until He comes back. This is the Christ whom we must experience, and this is the Christ whom we enjoy.

CHAPTER FIVE

THE BELIEVERS' ORGANIC UNION WITH CHRIST

Scripture Reading: 1 Cor. 15:45b; John 20:22; 3:5-6, 15, 36a; Rom. 6:3, 5; 1 Cor. 6:17; Rom. 8:9-11; 2 Tim. 4:22; Eph. 3:16-17; Col. 1:18a; Eph. 5:30; 2:15; Col. 3:10-11

RECEIVING THE REVELATION CONCERNING THE BELIEVERS' ORGANIC UNION WITH CHRIST

The secret of experiencing Christ is first to receive three revelations. The first is the revelation of Christ's Person, and the second is the revelation of Christ's work. These two revelations have been adequately covered in the previous chapters. In this chapter we come to the third revelation, the revelation concerning the believers' organic union with Christ. This organic union is the most crucial aspect of the secret of experiencing Christ. For us to experience Christ and enjoy Him, we must see a clear vision concerning our organic union with Him.

The Bible first reveals to us the Person of Christ, and then it reveals to us the work of Christ. After these two basic revelations, the Bible reveals to us the organic union which we have with Christ. In one of the first four books of the New Testament, the Gospel of John, we see an illustration of the vine with all the branches. Then in the following twenty-three books, from Acts through Revelation, what is revealed is mainly this organic union. Paul's fourteen Epistles especially focus on this one thing. The more we read Romans, 1 and 2 Corinthians, Galatians, Ephesians, Philippians, and Colossians, the more we can realize that Paul had seen a full revelation, and that he had a full knowledge concerning this revelation which unveils to us our organic union with Christ.

A UNION OF LIFE

The most wonderful reality in the Christian experience is that all the believers in Christ are united with Him in the way of life. The union of the believers with Christ is not by organization, but by life; hence, this union is organic. The word *organic* denotes that this union is absolutely a matter of life.

A good illustration of this organic union is our physical body. Our body has many members, but all the members are organically united into one body. The uniting factor is life. When the body dies, after a certain number of days all the members will be separated and scattered. When life is in the body, all the members are organically united together, but when life is gone, all the members eventually become disunited, detached. The members of the body are united together not by organization, but by a living, crucial, and vital factor—life. We the believers in Christ are one with Him because of such a living, uniting factor. For this reason we refer to our union with Christ as an organic union. In this message I would like to impress you with the fact that we have such an organic union with Christ.

Christ is wonderful in His Person, and He is excellent in His work. In His Person, He is both the complete God and the perfect man. In His work, He did everything that is needed for the fulfilling of God's purpose, and He did everything that is needed for our benefit. Whatever He is and whatever He has done is altogether for one thing: that He could be united to us organically. This wonderful organic union is very much neglected by most Christians today. Today's Christianity has become a religion, a religious organization, full of teachings, doctrines, ordinances, and practices, a religion which neglects the matter of life. Many Christians preach Christ and teach Christ in an objective way, making Him an objective Redeemer and an objective Savior. In their concept and realization Christ is in the third heavens, not within them. They may be right to a certain extent in an objective way, but surely they are wrong in relation to the subjective reality. Today in the Lord's recovery, the Lord is recovering this neglected matter of the believers' organic union with Christ.

A GRAFTED LIFE

The Bible is a wonderful book. It is wonderful not only in revealing Christ's Person and work, but it is even more wonderful in its revelation of this organic union. In the Old Testament there are thirty-nine books, and in the New Testament there are twenty-seven. In the four Gospels we cannot see a full revelation of this organic union. However, the organic union is strongly stressed in John chapters fourteen through seventeen. The central thought and focus of John 14 through 17 is this organic union. In chapter fifteen the Lord Jesus illustrated this organic union by saying that He is the vine and we, the believers in Him, are all the branches of this vine. Between the vine and the branches there is an organic union.

In John 15 we see the vine with all the branches, but we do not see that all the branches have been grafted into the vine. Originally, we, the believers in Christ, were not united to Christ. According to the picture in Romans 11:17 and 24, we were branches of a wild olive tree. But when we believed in the Lord Jesus, we were saved and we were regenerated. In regeneration we received a new life, and this new life made us alive. This new life also grafted us into Christ. We who formerly were branches of a wild olive tree have all been regenerated and made alive, and we all have been grafted into the cultivated olive tree, which is Christ with God's chosen people given to Him as His members. Originally, we were not branches in Christ, but we have been grafted into Christ. By our natural birth we were not branches of Christ, but through regeneration we were cut off from the wild olive tree and were grafted into the cultivated tree, which is Christ with His members as the divine organism to express the Triune God. Now between Christ, the cultivated tree, and us, the grafted branches, there is an organic union. This grafted life between the grafted branches and the cultivated tree is the best illustration of our organic union with Christ.

CHRIST BECOMING THE LIFE-GIVING SPIRIT TO ENTER INTO HIS BELIEVERS

After passing through the first four major processes of

incarnation, human living, crucifixion, and resurrection, Christ in His resurrection became a life-giving Spirit (1 Cor. 15:45b). This wonderful Man is the complete God and also the perfect man. Furthermore, He has done everything for God and for us. Eventually, in His resurrection He became a life-giving Spirit. This life-giving Spirit is the extract of His Person and His work. In making a medicine we may collect a number of elements from various plants, flowers, roots, and trees, and combine them together. We may then process these elements further and extract the crucial essence of each element to formulate the most effective medicine. This medicine may be a liquid, or it may be in the form of pills. In one drop of that liquid, or in one pill, we have the extract of many elements. This extract may be called the spirit of all those elements. In this extract is the crucial essence of all the elements. After passing through all the processes in His humanity, Christ as the last Adam became a life-giving Spirit. This life-giving Spirit can be considered as the extract of Christ in His Person and His work. In this life-giving Spirit, or in this extract, we have divinity, humanity, human living, the effectiveness of Christ's all-inclusive death, and the power of Christ's resurrection. The ascension of Christ is also included in this life-giving Spirit.

In His resurrection Christ became such a life-giving Spirit in order that He might enter into His believers (John 20:22). Today, anywhere on this earth, wherever and whenever a person calls on the name of the Lord Jesus, believes in Him, and receives Him as his Savior, this life-giving Spirit immediately enters into him. This means that Christ as the life-giving Spirit enters into His believers. Have you believed in the Lord Jesus? Have you called on His name and received Him? If so, you should realize that He has entered into your innermost being. He is the Almighty God, the Almighty Creator, and He became a perfect man. As such a One He accomplished everything. He died for us, He was buried, and He was resurrected. In His resurrection He was transfigured into the life-giving Spirit. Now this life-giving Spirit is not restricted by anything. He is not limited by time or by space. He is everywhere, He is present, and He is now. In the morning, at noon, in the evening, or at midnight, He is always now, and He is always present. He is present with you just like the air. Wherever you go there is air. Air is always now, and air is always present. Whenever you open your mouth, air gets into you. Often you are unconscious of the fact that the air has entered into you. This is why Romans 10:8 tells us that Christ as the living Word is near you, even in your mouth and in your heart.

I do not deny that Christ is great. On one hand He is still on the throne in the third heavens (Rom. 8:34; Col. 3:1). There in the third heavens He is the Lord of all and the Administrator of the entire universe. He is the great God and the great Lord. Yet, on the other hand, He is the Spirit. As the life-giving Spirit He is everywhere. Whenever we call on Him, He enters into us. Now He is within us. Hallelujah for this!

CHRIST AS THE LIFE-GIVING SPIRIT REGENERATING THE BELIEVERS IN THEIR SPIRIT

As the life-giving Spirit, Christ has regenerated the believers in their spirit (John 3:5-6). Doctrinally, it is difficult to explain how Christ, after entering into us, regenerates us in our spirit. However, in experience it is simple. When a sinner repents, confesses his sins, believes in the Lord Jesus, and calls on His name, at that very moment Christ as the life-giving Spirit enters into his spirit to enliven his dead spirit, that is, to regenerate him in his spirit. Immediately such a person becomes alive, happy, and joyful. He cannot explain what has happened to him, but he is rejoicing. He may continue to repent of his sins for the remainder of the day. A great change has taken place in his life. This sinner has been saved. He has been regenerated, and he is now a Christian. I believe that many of us have had this kind of experience. This is what it means to be saved, to be regenerated, and to be converted.

THE BELIEVERS BEING BROUGHT INTO AN ORGANIC UNION WITH CHRIST

Through their believing in Christ and their being baptized into Christ, the believers have been brought into an organic union with Christ (John 3:15, 36a; Rom. 6:3, 5). When we believed in Christ and were baptized into Him, an organic union took place in our being. This organic union which took place at our believing in Jesus has united us to Christ. In other words, this union has grafted us into Christ, who is the vine tree. It is by such a transaction that we have been made branches of Christ. Hallelujah, we are believers in Christ, and we are branches grafted into this wonderful, universal vine tree! This is the organic union.

THE BELIEVERS' REGENERATED SPIRIT
AND CHRIST AS THE LIFE-GIVING SPIRIT
JOINED TO BE ONE SPIRIT

The believers' regenerated spirit and Christ who is the life-giving Spirit are joined to be one spirit (1 Cor. 6:17). This is wonderful. We, the believers in Christ, all have a regenerated spirit. Our spirit was dead, but through believing in Christ it has been made alive (Eph. 2:1). Now we all have within us our own spirit which has been regenerated and made alive. At the same time Christ as the life-giving Spirit is within our spirit. These two spirits are joined to be one spirit. This is a most mysterious and wonderful thing. Most Christians today have no concept of this mysterious and wonderful reality. But in the Lord's recovery this is stressed day after day. That our spirit is joined to Christ, the life-giving Spirit, as one spirit is a most crucial and vital matter. This is the ultimate consummation of the organic union which we have with Christ. No union could be more intimate than this union.

The realization that we are one spirit with Christ will cause us to be beside ourselves with joy. Such a realization may cause us to shout, "Hallelujah, we are one spirit with the Lord!" Many times I have been asked how I, as an elderly man, could be so active and so energetic. My secret is that I am one spirit with the Lord. Today, many toys are made to operate by electricity. It is electricity which makes them so active. Because we are one spirit with Christ, we have the heavenly, divine electricity energizing us continually. How we need to realize our organic union with Christ and live in this reality!

CHRIST AS THE LIFE-GIVING SPIRIT
INDWELLING THE BELIEVERS IN THEIR SPIRIT

Christ as the life-giving Spirit indwells the believers in their spirit. First, as the life-giving Spirit, Christ regenerated us in our spirit. Now He dwells in our spirit (Rom. 8:9-11; 2 Tim. 4:22). It is a wonderful fact that Christ is not only in us, but He also dwells in us.

For a person to dwell in a room means that he occupies it and fills it with his activities. Moreover, a person accomplishes many of his intentions in his own home. Although I have a very adequate office in which to do my work, I do not like to work there; rather, I like to work in my home. While I am dwelling in my home, I work. The Lord Jesus today only has a home; He does not have an office. His home is His office. The Lord's office is within us. Many of us may realize that the Lord Jesus has made us His home, but not many realize that, as the Lord's home, we are also His office.

The Lord Jesus not only dwells in us as His home, but He also works within us. He is carrying out all His work within us. Because He has many things to do within us, He is working in us twenty-four hours a day. We all need to realize that today the Lord Jesus indwells us, making us His home and also His office. He is working within us as His office. What a wonderful thought this is! Our Lord dwells in us, and while He dwells in us, He works. He has made us His home and His office as well. This is the organic union which we have with Christ. We all need to know Christ in such a living way.

CHRIST MAKING HIS HOME
IN THE BELIEVERS' HEARTS

Christ is making His home in the believers' hearts through the Spirit's strengthening them into their spirit, that is, into their inner man (Eph. 3:16-17). The strangest thing, and also the sweetest and most enjoyable thing, is that within us, the believers in Christ, there is always a kind of strengthening. Continually, both day and night, we are being strengthened from within. It is this inward strengthening which enables us to say, "Lord Jesus, I love You. Lord, occupy me and fill me up. I desire to be possessed and taken over by You. I want to be

fully occupied by You. Lord, I simply want to be one with You."
We fail to realize that this strengthening has a direction, that
is, that Christ would make His own home in our entire being.
By this inward strengthening, gradually we will say, "Lord
Jesus, fill me with Yourself and possess me in my mind, my
emotions, and my will. Fill and possess me in every part, in
every avenue, of my inward being." This is to allow Christ to
make His home in our whole being. This is the fullness of the
organic union which we have with Christ, a union in which
we are fully united with Christ in an organic way.

CHRIST AS THE HEAD OF THE BODY AND
THE BELIEVERS AS THE MEMBERS OF THE BODY
BEING JOINED TOGETHER TO BE
THE GREAT, UNIVERSAL NEW MAN

Eventually, Christ as the Head of the Body (Col. 1:18a)
and the believers as the members of the Body (Eph. 5:30) are
joined together to be the great, universal new man (Eph. 2:15;
Col. 3:10-11). In the organic union, Christ becomes the Head
of the universal new man, and we the believers all are the
members of this great, universal new man. He is the Head
and we all are the members. He and we, we and He, are
organically united together to be one complete and perfect
universal new man. In such an organic union we live together
with Him, move together with Him, and work together with
Him. Christ and we have only one purpose, one goal, and one
aim. This is the ultimate consummation in full of our organic
union with Him.

CHAPTER SIX

ABIDING IN CHRIST

Scripture Reading: John 15:4-5, 7-8; 1 John 2:27-28, 21-23;
Col. 2:4, 8; 1 Tim. 1:3-4; Eph. 4:14; 1 John 2:16; James 4:1, 3;
Phil. 4:6; 2:14; Eph. 4:26, 31; Gal. 5:2-4; Col. 2:20-21; 1 John
1:2-3; 4:8, 16; 1:5-7; 2:6; 3:24; 4:15-16; John 14:23; Rom. 6:5;
Eph. 4:15; Col. 2:7; 1 Cor. 3:6; John 15:8

In the previous chapter we saw our organic union with
Christ. In this organic union we are actually one with Christ
in the Spirit. Based upon this union, the New Testament tells
us that we need to abide in Christ. The Gospel of John tells us
that Christ is the vine and we are the branches (John 15:5).
As the branches we should abide in Christ as the vine all the
time. The branches and the vine not only give us a good illustration of the organic union, but they also illustrate how the
branches abide in the vine. When the branches abide in
the vine, the vine also abides in the branches. This mutual
abiding actually causes the vine and the branches to grow.
The growth of the entire vine depends upon this abiding.
Christ is the vine, and we are His branches. For us to grow
in Him and for Him to grow in us, we need to abide in Him.
The matter of abiding in Christ is a central teaching in the
New Testament, especially in the writings of John and Paul.
The foundation of this teaching of abiding is in John 15. Then
Paul in his Epistles goes on to develop this teaching of abiding.

REMAINING IN CHRIST
AND NOT BEING DISTRACTED FROM HIM

To abide in Christ is to remain in Him. All the branches
abiding in a vine remain in it. Once a branch is removed, it
dies. On the one hand the tree must support the branches,

and on the other hand the branches must remain in the tree. As believers, we should remain in Christ, but there are many things that would distract us from Him. Therefore, in order to remain in Christ we must avoid being distracted by any of these things.

By Heresies

The first category of things that can distract us from Christ is heresies. Some of the teachings among Christians today are good, but some are heretical. One of the greatest heresies today is a movement whose founder claims to be another Christ. He says that Jesus Christ was defeated, but he will be victorious. What a great heresy this is! Anyone who would accept this kind of heresy would surely be distracted from Christ. We must not be distracted from Christ but rather remain in Christ. First John 2:21 says, "I have not written to you because you do not know the truth, but because you know it, and because no lie is of the truth." The word truth in John's writings refers to Christ as the reality of the Triune God, and the lie refers to a teaching denying this truth of Christ being the reality of the Triune God. First John 2:22 says, "Who is the liar if not he who is denying that Jesus is the Christ? This is the antichrist, who is denying the Father and the Son." At John's time, there were some who taught that Jesus was an earthly man, the son of Joseph and Mary, and that Christ was another person. These were heretics who taught that Jesus was not the Christ. In this verse John says that whoever denies that Jesus is the Christ is an antichrist. Such a person is anti-Christ, that is, against Christ. To deny that Jesus is the Christ is to deny the Father and the Son. If you say that Jesus is not the Christ, then you deny both the Father and the Son because the Triune God is one. The New Testament tells us that Jesus is the Christ, that Christ is the Son of God, and that this Son of God is always together with the Father and one with the Father (Matt. 16:13, 16; John 16:32; 10:30). If you say that Jesus is not the Christ, that means you deny Christ. If you deny Christ, you deny the Son of God and you also deny the Father who is one with the Son. This is surely a heresy.

Verse 23 says, "Everyone who denies the Son does not have the Father either; he who confesses the Son has the Father also." This verse also shows that the Father is one with the Son. If you have the Son, then you have the Father. But if you deny the Son, you reject the Father, and you have neither the Son nor the Father. On the positive side, he who confesses the Son has the Father also. If we confess the Son, then we have the Father also. This is the truth. To deny the Son is a heresy. Such a heresy distracts the believers from Christ.

By Philosophy, Tradition, and Teachings Other Than God's Economy

Another category of distractions from Christ is philosophy (Col. 2:4, 8). Philosophy in Colossians 2 refers to the ancient Greek philosophy. As early as the first century this kind of philosophy invaded the church. Heresies came mainly from the Jews, while philosophy came mainly from the Greeks. It is the subtlety of the enemy Satan to bring in these things among Christians to distract them from Christ.

Traditions are also a distraction from Christ. In the first century there were Jewish traditions and also Greek traditions. Wherever the gospel goes, those who hear it have their own kind of tradition. All such traditions distract believers from Christ.

Another category of distractions from Christ is teachings other than God's economy. In 1 Timothy 1:3-4 Paul tells us that we must avoid the teachings which differ from God's economy. In the human thought there are many different kinds of teachings. The good teachings as well as the bad teachings distract us from Christ. The teachings of Confucius are good, but in China those teachings have distracted many learned people from Christ. At the apostles' time the Jews had many teachings from the thirty-nine books of the Old Testament. After the churches were established, these Jewish teachings entered into the church life. There was a strong invasion of the Jewish teachings and the Greek philosophy into the church life. Both the Jewish teachings and the Greek philosophy distracted the early Christians from Christ. These are some of the winds of teaching which Paul refers to in Ephesians 4:14. Through the past twenty centuries many teachings have become winds to blow Christians away from Christ. For example, the Catholic Church teaches people to worship the "holy mother" instead of worshipping God and Christ directly. They teach people to pray to Mary, and then Mary will carry their prayer to God. What a distraction this is! This teaching is a great heresy. However, even some teachings which seem to be quite good may distract people from Christ. In order for us to remain in Christ, we must stay away from all heresies, philosophies, traditions, and even from so many good teachings which are not concerning God's New Testament economy.

By the Lust of the Flesh, the Lust of the Eyes, the Vainglory of Life, and Pleasures

As mentioned in 1 John 2:16, another category of things that would easily distract us from Christ includes the lust of the flesh, the lust of the eyes, and the vainglory of life. We are all people in the flesh, and in our flesh there are many lusts. Therefore, we must be very watchful lest at any time, any lust may rise up from our flesh to carry us away from Christ. Besides the lust of the flesh there is the lust of the eyes. In 1933 I went to Shanghai for the first time. In that large city the church had two meeting halls, one on the west side of the city and the other on the north side. While going between the two halls to speak, I traveled down Nanking Road which was lined with department stores having large show windows. Even at midnight the show windows were brightly lit. After looking at the displays many things came into my mind, and by the time I reached the other hall I found it difficult to speak the word as a message from my spirit. The show windows in the department stores stir up the lust of the eyes. Whenever you look at all the displays in the department store, it seems that your spirit is gone. It seems that Christ is in the heavens and you are in hell. By window-shopping in this way many people indulge the lust of their eyes.

This verse also mentions the vainglory of this life. To have a big house and a better car is a vainglory. To have a big car to show off is the vainglory of this life. These three things—the lust of the flesh, the lust of the eyes, and the vainglory of this life—all distract us from Christ.

James 4:1 and 3 mention pleasures as another category of distractions from Christ. Drinking, eating, sight-seeing, and certain kinds of music are pleasures which can distract us from Christ.

By Anxiety, Murmuring, Anger, and Any Agitation

Another big distraction is anxiety. Anxiety is like a little demon always bothering us. Who could live even one day without any kind of anxiety? Very often wives are anxious concerning their husbands. From the day of her engagement a wife may begin to be anxious about whether her husband will be faithful to her or not. Once this anxiety enters into her, it will never leave her. After marriage, a husband and wife may have some children. From the first day their little child is born, they may be anxious whether this child will breathe well, sleep well, and eat well. The parents are anxious for their children from the time of their birth to the time they themselves have children. They are anxious to see whether their children will read well, study well, get the best grades, and graduate from the best university. Then they become anxious concerning their children's marriages. After the children's marriages they are anxious concerning the grandchildren. This human life is full of anxiety, and this anxiety keeps us away from Christ.

In Philippians, a book on enjoying Christ, Paul tells us, "Be anxious for nothing" (4:6). That means we should not worry about anything. But we all have some worries. Sometimes when we do not have much anxiety today, we borrow the anxiety of tomorrow. Very often we borrow anxiety from tomorrow. Tomorrow has not yet come, yet we borrow tomorrow's anxiety. We human beings are just people of anxiety. But once you have anxiety, you are cut off from Christ. It is not easy to get rid of anxiety. The best way to get rid of anxiety is to tell your need to God (Phil. 4:6). Do not worry for anything, but rather unload your care (1 Pet. 5:7). You need to charge your anxiety to God. To say this is easy, but to practice not having anxiety is very difficult.

Besides anxiety, another distraction is murmuring (Phil. 2:14). Every married person has murmured about his husband or wife at some time. Even in the church life there may be some murmuring. The brothers may murmur about the elders, and the sisters may murmur about the brothers. The young ones may murmur about the older ones, and the older ones may murmur about the young ones. Anxiety and murmuring are two things that so easily keep us away from Christ. Philippians is a book on the experience of Christ. This experience is quite often frustrated by these two things, anxiety and murmuring. Hence, the Apostle Paul exhorts us concerning both.

Anger and any kind of agitation also cut us off from the experience of Christ (Eph. 4:26, 31). We all are too easily agitated. Sometimes just a little word will agitate us. Both the young people and the older ones are very easily agitated. But any time you are agitated by anything or by anyone, you are distracted from Christ.

Anger is an issue of agitation. Although it cannot be considered as sin, it surely distracts us from experiencing Christ in our daily life. Therefore, the Apostle exhorts us not to remain in anger to the point where it becomes sin (Eph. 4:26).

By Culture, Religion, Ethics, Morality, and Character-Improving

Another category of distractions includes culture, religion, ethics, morality, and character-improving. Character-improving seems to be quite good. Although it is good, it is nevertheless a problem, for if you try to improve your character, this character-improving will distract you from enjoying Christ. This means that you pay your attention to your character rather than to Christ. Therefore, character-improving is also a distraction from Christ.

We may also be distracted by trying to do good. I do not mean that we do not need to do good, but trying to do good distracts us from Christ. Trying to be spiritual, scriptural, holy, and victorious also distracts us from Christ. While we are trying to be these things, we are distracted. This means that we should not be people of culture, religion, ethics, or morality. Neither should we be people of character-improving, doing good, or trying to be spiritual, scriptural, holy, and victorious. We should only be people of Christ! Our entire being—our thought, our consideration, our feeling, our every part—must be filled and saturated with Christ and we should only care for experiencing Christ. I do not mean that we should be wild, evil, or careless. I mean that we should not be occupied by any good thing other than Christ, nor should we care for anything other than the experience of Christ. This is not my teaching. This is the very thing that I have quoted from the New Testament. After studying the New Testament for many years I eventually realized that it requires us to drop all things other than Christ Himself and to remain in Christ because Christ is much higher and better than all culture, religion, ethics, morality, and character-improving. He is the most excellent among all things for us to apprehend and experience. Do not stay in anything other than Christ, no matter how good it may be. Do not remain in even the best thing, but rather remain in Christ all the time.

REMAINING IN THE FELLOWSHIP OF THE DIVINE LIFE

In Message Five of the Life-study of 1 John we pointed out that, because we have received the divine life, we have been brought into the divine fellowship. This divine fellowship is just the flow of the divine life. With electricity there is a current which supplies all the electrical appliances. Every appliance should remain in the electrical current to receive the supply of electricity. Within us there is a current of the divine life. In order for us to enjoy Christ and experience Him, we must remain in this current of the divine life. When we remain in the current of the divine life, we touch God as the source. This is fully taught by John in his first Epistle. First John tells us that the Apostles preached, or ministered, the divine life to us (1 John 1:2-3). After we receive this divine life, we are in the divine fellowship. We should remain in this fellowship to touch God and enjoy Him as the very source of grace and truth. In this fellowship we realize that God is love and that God is light (1 John 4:8, 16; 1:5-7). The divine love is the source of grace, and the divine light is the source of truth. It is when we are touching the source that we enjoy Christ. We enjoy God as love and light in Christ, and this results in our enjoyment of Christ as grace and truth.

This is the secret of experiencing Christ. In 2 Corinthians 13:14 Paul says, "The grace of the Lord Jesus Christ, and the love of God, and the fellowship of the Holy Spirit be with you all." This is to enjoy the Triune God by remaining in the divine fellowship that we may touch the Triune God as the source. When we touch the Triune God as the source, as love and light, we enjoy the riches of Christ as grace and truth, and we experience Christ in the fellowship of the Holy Spirit as the transmission. This is the enjoyment of grace and truth. In this enjoyment we realize that the source is God's love and God's light. All of this can be fully proven by our own experiences.

ABIDING, DWELLING, AND MAKING HOME IN CHRIST

To abide in Christ is not only to remain in Him, but also to dwell in Him. To dwell in Him means to make your home in Him. Most English readers understand the word abide to mean simply to remain. But the Greek word for abide means to make home. In John 14:23 the same Greek root is used in the nominative form. Used as a noun, this word means an abode, a dwelling place, a home. Therefore, the Greek word for abide does not mean simply to remain, but also to dwell, to make home.

To abide in Christ is not only to remain in Him, but to be fully settled in Him. Sometimes when I visit the churches I stay in the church guest house. Although I may stay there for a time, I do not make my home there. I stay there with the expectation that I will leave after a few days. Our abiding in Christ should not be like this, but rather like our dwelling in our own home. If you abide in a certain place for a few days and then leave, that is not a home to you, but a hotel or a motel. Unfortunately, many Christians abide in Christ as a motel, just for a temporary stay. But we need to get ourselves settled in Christ, to make Christ our home. We need to dwell in Him. In John 14:23 the Lord Jesus said, "If anyone loves

Me, he will keep My word, and My Father will love him, and We will come to him and make an abode with him." This verse says that both the Father and the Son will come to us and make an abode with us. For the Father and the Son to make an abode with us means that the Triune God settles in us, making us His abode, that we would make Him our abode. The abode in John 14:23 and in 1 John 2:6, 3:24, and 4:15-16 is a mutual abode. God takes us as His abode, and we take Him as our abode. Our real and permanent home is our God. Christ is our home and our dwelling place.

GROWING IN CHRIST

Finally, to abide in Christ is to grow in Christ. If you take Christ as your home, He will eventually become the soil to you. Look at the branches abiding in the vine. The vine is a home to the branches, and at the same time the vine is the soil to the branches. While the branches are abiding in the vine, they are also rooting into the soil (Col. 2:7). Therefore, they all are growing (1 Cor. 3:6; Eph. 4:15). The vine and the branches in John 15 are not an illustration of a dead, lifeless home. The abode in John 15 is an organic home because all the dwellers are fruitbearing branches (John 15:5). That the branches bear fruit indicates that they are growing. While we are abiding in Christ, we are growing. This is the way to experience Christ, to enjoy Him, and to grow in Him and with Him. While we are growing in Him and He is growing in us, there is a kind of mutual growing (Rom. 6:5). This is the enjoyment of Christ, and this is the real experience of Christ. I hope that we all would practice abiding in Christ.

CHAPTER SEVEN

LIVING CHRIST

Scripture Reading: John 14:19; Gal. 2:20a; Col. 3:4a; John 6:57b; Gal. 2:19; Phil. 3:9; 1:19-21a; 2:12-13, 15-16; 4:8-9, 12-13; Rom. 8:4

In the previous chapters we have seen Christ's Person, Christ's work, and our organic union with Him. For us to experience Christ, we need to see who He is and what He has done for us. He is the complete God and the perfect man, and He has done everything for us. As such a wonderful Person who has accomplished all the excellent things for us, He became a life-giving Spirit. The life-giving Spirit is the totality of His Person and His work. In this life-giving Spirit is the Person of Christ and everything He has accomplished for us. All the elements of His wonderful Person and His excellent work are condensed and compounded into this life-giving Spirit. When we believed in Him and called on His name, He came into our spirit as the all-inclusive life-giving Spirit. Now within us there is an organic union. It is in this organic union that Christ lives in us and we live in Him. This is the subjective experience of Christ.

RECOVERING THE SUBJECTIVE EXPERIENCE OF CHRIST

Many Christians experience Christ only in an objective way. However, the holy Word reveals that there are two aspects of our experience of Christ. With everything in the universe, there are always two aspects, two sides. Even a very thin piece of paper has two sides. When you look at one side, it may be blank, but when you turn to the other side, you may see a composition written there. If you concentrate only on the blank side, you will miss a great deal. In the same way, it is possible for us to completely miss the subjective side of the experience of Christ by concentrating only on the objective side.

On the objective side, Christ was God. Then He became a man, lived on this earth, went to the cross, died for us, and was buried. He rose from the dead and ascended to the heavens where He is now on the throne at the right hand of God. He is in the heavens waiting for a time when He can come back and set up His kingdom to rule over this earth. At that time He will close the old dispensation and bring in the new heaven and new earth with the holy city, New Jerusalem, and all of us who have believed in Him will be with Him there for eternity. This is the objective side of experiencing Christ presented in the Bible.

According to the objective teaching concerning the experience of Christ, we worship God as though we are far away from Him. We believe that the Lord Jesus is our Savior who died for our sins, and that God forgives us because of Jesus Christ. Then we try to do good to please God and glorify Him, and finally one day we will die and go to a prepared place. When Jesus returns, He will raise us up from the dead and take us to be with Him where we will enjoy eternal blessing with Him for eternity. With this objective view we cannot see that Christ and we, we and Christ, have an organic union. It seems that Christ has never been united to us, and that we have never been united to Him. He lived apart from us and accomplished everything apart from us. We believe in Him and accept Him altogether in an objective way—He is He, and we are we. It seems that there is no union between Christ and us. Objectively, this may be right, but subjectively, it is absolutely lacking and altogether wrong.

Consider our physical being. We have skin, flesh, and bones; we have many physical parts which are touchable and visible. Yet, this is merely the outermost part of our being. Inside of our body there is a life which is invisible and untouchable. However, although this life is intangible, it is the most crucial part of our human being. Without this crucial part we would be like a lifeless machine or a robot.

Today's objective teaching is too superficial; it has made many Christians like robots or machines in their spiritual life. Many do not know how to fellowship with the Lord or how to experience and enjoy the Lord in the fellowship of the Spirit, and they do not know that the Lord today is one with them in their spirit. They fail to see the two aspects of the Lord's being.

Christ is the King of all, the Lord of all, and even the Head of all in the heavens. He is sitting there on the throne exercising His authority to rule the entire universe. However, this is just one side. On the other side, through His death and resurrection He became a life-giving Spirit (1 Cor. 15:45). Today Christ is the Lord, the King, and the Head objectively, far away from us. As such a One He is great, marvelous, high, and dignified. But in this aspect we cannot experience Him. He is there in the heavens, yet we cannot touch Him. But, hallelujah, He has another aspect. He became a life-giving Spirit. The word for spirit in both Hebrew and Greek also means air. Today, Christ is just like the air. Hallelujah, He is the life-giving air!

We all know that physical air gives us life. If there were no air, after a few minutes all of us would be dead. We live by breathing; we live by the air. Today the Lord Jesus is our air. John 20:20 tells us that on the day of the Lord's resurrection He came back to the disciples. They were not expecting Him. As they met together, they were fully disappointed, thinking that the Lord Jesus had left them. To their great surprise, all of a sudden the Lord Jesus was there. Then the Lord breathed on them and told them to receive the holy air, the Holy Spirit (John 20:22). He breathed on them to bring in more air.

In Greek the word for air, for Spirit, and for breath is *pneuma*. When I was a young man living in north China, not many of the young people there knew English. An agent of Chevrolet began to sell automobiles in China, and since they needed some young people who knew English, they asked me to be their agent. As I looked at one of the cars, I saw the word PNEUMATIC printed on the tires in large English letters. Although I knew English, when I read this word, I said, "What is this? Pneumatic?" Later I learned that it meant to be full of air. A tire needs to be full of air; otherwise, it becomes flat. No one desires to have a flat tire. However, spiritually speaking, when we are short of the Spirit, we are like a flat tire. We are not pneumatic because we lack the spiritual air. Many Christians do not see that Jesus Christ today is the life-giving *pneuma*. He is very pneumatic, and when we are filled with Him, we also become pneumatic, full of air. When the tires of your car are short of *pneuma,* you go to the gas station to get more air. Then the tires are full of air. In a spiritual sense, we need to check ourselves, whether we are pneumatic or a flat tire. I can testify that I am pneumatic; I am full of air. We should not be Christians who are short of air; we should be pneumatic Christians. Not only every day, but every second, we must breathe in Christ.

In our hymnal we selected about 800 hymns from over 10,000 collected hymns. Among these selected hymns were a number of hymns written by A.B. Simpson, the founder of the Christian and Missionary Alliance. One of his hymns (*Hymns,* #255) speaks of breathing in the Lord. The first stanza and chorus of this hymn say:

> O Lord, breathe Thy Spirit on me
>   Teach me how to breathe Thee in;
> Help me pour into Thy bosom
>   All my life of self and sin.

> I am breathing out my sorrow,
>   Breathing out my sin;
> I am breathing, breathing, breathing,
>   All Thy fulness in.

After singing this hymn for the first time, one brother was offended at the thought of breathing the Lord. However, a few years later, after having had the experience of breathing Christ, he expressed his appreciation of this hymn.

The Lord's recovery is to recover all the subjective experiences of Christ. This is why in the previous chapters after I presented to you many items of Christ's Person and work, I emphasized the fact that now there is an organic union between us and Christ. This organic union is not physical. It is not material, visible, or touchable. It is something organic, something of life. No life, whether animal, vegetable, human, or divine, is visible. Life is real, but life is invisible. Electricity is a good illustration of this. Electricity is not visible, but it is real. All the tubes in a fluorescent light fixture are united to the power plant in a kind of electrical union. It is this electrical union which affords the light. This electrical union is the electrical current flowing between the power plant and the fluorescent tubes.

We may apply this illustration to understand our organic union with Christ. We are the fluorescent tubes, and Christ is the power plant. Between us and Christ there is a spiritual current. This spiritual current is an organic union. We are united to Christ and Christ is united to us in this current. In this organic union, Christ is in you, in me, and in every one of His believers. This is the organic union in which we should abide, in which we should remain. To abide in Christ is to remain in this organic union. Every day, morning and evening, we have the deep sense that in our spirit there is a kind of current flowing. This is the living Christ, this is the organic union, and this is the spiritual fellowship of the divine life. Christ lives in this organic union, and we also live in this organic union. He and we are living together in this one organic union.

This organic union is fully illustrated by Christ in John 15. There He told us that He is the vine and we are the branches of this vine. In the vine with all the branches we can see an organic union in which life is flowing and circulating. It is in this circulation that both the vine and the branches grow. The vine and the branches are growing together in this organic union. We are living together with Christ. Christ lives and we live with Him. The vine lives in all the branches, and all the branches live in the vine. They live together one with another. We all need to see this.

CHRIST LIVING IN RESURRECTION AND IN US

Christ lives in resurrection, and He lives within us. This is clearly indicated in John 14:19 and Galatians 2:20. In Galatians 2:20 Paul says, "It is no longer I who live, but

Christ lives in me." Oh, Christ lives in us! He *sits* on the throne as the Lord, but He *lives* in our hearts as the Spirit. In John 14:19, the Lord Jesus said that because He lives, that is, in resurrection, we shall live also in Him. As the vine lives in the branches, the branches also live. We all need to be deeply impressed that Christ lives in us and we live in Him. How wonderful this is!

CHRIST BEING OUR LIFE, AND WE LIVING BY HIM THROUGH ENJOYING HIM

Christ is our life, and we live by Him through enjoying Him. In Colossians 3:4 we are told that Christ is our life, and in John 6:57, that if we eat Him, we shall live because of Him. Christ is not only our life, but also our life supply. He is the bread of life (John 6:48). Bread is something for us to eat. We live by what we eat. If we did not eat, how could we live? We live by eating. At times I become tired, but always after eating a good meal, I am nourished. I live by what I eat. In a spiritual sense, we live by eating Jesus. Just as a car runs by the gasoline it "eats," we "run" by eating Jesus. Jesus is our food and Jesus is our "gasoline." We live by Him through enjoying Him. For this reason, every day we need some time to contact the Lord. We should not say that we are too busy to eat. If we refrain from eating, after a certain period of time we will die. We can never graduate from eating. The more we eat Jesus, the better. We eat Jesus, and we live by Him.

HAVING DIED TO THE LAW THAT WE MIGHT LIVE TO GOD

In Galatians 2:19 Paul says that we have died to the law that we might live to God. Although this verse is in the Bible, we may be unaware of it. When we read the law, the Ten Commandments in the Bible, and realize that it is good, we may determine to keep it. However, Paul says that we Christians have died to the law. The law is good, but it is not for us to keep. We have died to the law that we might live to God. This means that we are not responsible to the law, but we are responsible to Christ. We are responsible to our God, who is Christ.

Let me illustrate in this way. Suppose you read in the Bible, "Honor thy father and thy mother" (Exo. 20:12). You may say to yourself, "I am a child of my parents, but I do not honor them all the time. Through reading the Bible I have learned that I should honor my parents." Immediately you may make a strong decision to honor your parents. You may tell the Lord, "Lord, You know that I am weak. I have the desire to honor my parents, but I cannot do it. Lord, help me to honor my parents." I prayed this kind of prayer many times. I can testify to you that this kind of prayer was never answered. The more you pray that the Lord will help you to honor your parents, the more you may lose your temper with your parents. When you read such a verse, you need to say, "Satan, let me tell you that I have died to the law, and I am not responsible to the law. I am living to God; I am living to Christ. I do not care for the Ten Commandments. I only care for Christ. He is within me. He lives within me and I live with Him. I am responsible only to Him. Morning and evening, day and night, every minute and every second, I am responsible to Christ. I live to Christ, I live by Christ, I live in Christ, I live with Christ, and I live Christ (Phil. 1:21a). I am one with Christ." Spontaneously, Christ in you will live to honor your parents. Now your honoring of your parents is not you, but Christ. It is not you who honor your parents; it is Christ in you who honors them. We all need to see this.

Many of God's people use the Bible in a wrong way. For example, many Christian husbands and wives misuse Ephesians 5:22 and 25. These verses say that wives should submit to their husbands, and that husbands should love their wives. However, each may read these verses for the other, not for himself. The husbands may read verse 22, "Wives, be subject to your own husbands, as to the Lord," while neglecting verse 25; and the wives may read verse 25, "Husbands, love your wives even as Christ also loved the church," while overlooking verse 22.

In the early years of my ministry a number of cases between husbands and wives were brought to me. Both the husband and the wife came to me to present their case. The husband complained that his wife was not submissive, and the wife, that her husband was not loving. In this way the Bible became the law for a lawsuit. But we need to see that we have died to the law. We no longer live to the law and are not responsible to the law. We live to Christ and are responsible to Him. We should no longer care about the law; we should only care for Christ. Our need is simply to pray, "Lord Jesus, I love You. Thank You, Lord, that You are one with me. You live in me and I live in You. Lord Jesus, it is not I, but You. I desire to live You every minute and every second." A wife who prays in this way will gradually find that she can easily submit herself to her husband. She will do it unconsciously, willingly, and unintentionally. It is the same with the husbands. There will be no need for the husbands to determine to love their wives; they will love their wives spontaneously. We have died to the law that we may live to Christ. This is to live Christ.

FOUND IN CHRIST

If you are a person who lives Christ, then everyone will find you in Christ. People will realize that you are a person in Christ, not in anything else. You live Christ, and you express Christ in your daily life; thus, what people see in you is Christ expressed by you. In Philippians 3:9 Paul expressed his desire to be found in Christ. He was a person who aspired to be found in Christ.

NOT HAVING OUR OWN RIGHTEOUSNESS WHICH IS OF THE LAW, BUT THE RIGHTEOUSNESS WHICH IS OF GOD AND WHICH IS CHRIST

If you are living Christ, you are a person absolutely in Christ. Whatever you do is Christ, and whatever you say is Christ. In this way Christ becomes your righteousness, which is considered in the Bible as God's righteousness. Christ is your love, kindness, and humility. Christ is everything in your virtues.

MAGNIFYING CHRIST BY THE BOUNTIFUL SUPPLY OF THE SPIRIT OF JESUS CHRIST

When we experience Christ to such an extent, we magnify

Christ, regardless of the environment, by the bountiful supply of the Spirit of Jesus Christ (Phil. 1:19-20). The Spirit of Jesus Christ is simply the life-giving Spirit, who is Jesus Christ Himself. In this all-inclusive life-giving Spirit is the bountiful supply for our daily life. It is by this bountiful supply that we magnify Christ.

WORKING OUT OUR OWN SALVATION BY LIVING CHRIST

In Philippians 2:12 we are told to work out our own salvation. The salvation spoken of here is not the salvation which saves us from perdition. Rather, it is the salvation which saves us from our daily problems. If, as a husband, I cannot love my wife, that is a real problem. And if, as a wife, you cannot submit yourself to your husband, that is also a problem. Not being able to control our temper is another problem. From these kinds of problems we all need a daily salvation. We ourselves work out this daily salvation by living Christ. By living Christ we are saved, not only from losing our temper, but from every kind of shortcoming and weakness. Living Christ saves us from every defect and makes us perfect. We all need to experience this daily, subjective salvation.

SHINING AS LUMINARIES, HOLDING FORTH THE WORD OF LIFE

If we experience such a daily salvation, we will shine as luminaries, as lights, in the world, holding forth the word of life (Phil. 2:15-16). Our living holds forth, presents to people, the word of life. On the one hand, we are preaching and teaching the word of life; on the other hand, we are presenting the living word of life by our living Christ. When we live Christ, we shine. We shine as the lights of Christ, and that shining presents to others the word of life.

EMPOWERED TO DO ALL THINGS BY LIVING CHRIST

If we live Christ, we shall be empowered to do all things (Phil. 4:13). To be empowered to do all things means to be strengthened to show forth all of the human virtues created by God for His expression. Genesis 1:26 tells us that God created man in His own image in order that man might express Him. The image of God refers to the divine attributes. With God there are the divine attributes, and with man there are the human virtues. God created man with human virtues. That is the reason man is ethical, moral, and good.

In Philippians 4:8 Paul refers to six virtues: "For the rest, brothers, whatever is true, whatever is honorable, whatever is righteous, whatever is pure, whatever is lovely, whatever is well-spoken of, if there is any virtue and if any praise, take account of these things." As a man, as a human being, you need to be true, honorable, righteous, pure, lovely, and well-spoken of. I repeat, every human being must be true, not false, and must be honorable and righteous. He must be right with God and with everyone, and he must be pure, lovely, and well-spoken of. He must have some virtue, and he must have something worthy of praise. As a human being you should be such a person. In Philippians Paul is instructing us how to live Christ. If we live Christ, we will be a person who is true, honorable, righteous, pure, lovely, well-spoken of, full of virtues, and full of things which are worthy of praise.

A human being should express God in all the human virtues which reflect all the divine attributes. However, man became fallen. The entire human race became the opposite of what God intended. Mankind became untrue, dishonorable, unrighteous, impure, unlovely, ill-spoken of, without virtue, and without anything worthy of praise. However, on the day we were saved, God in Christ came into us. This God now lives in us. If we live Christ, who is the embodiment of God, surely we will live a Person who is true, honorable, righteous, pure, lovely, well-spoken of, full of virtues, and worthy of praise. Although we should be such a person, in ourselves we cannot be. But in Philippians 4:13 Paul says, "I can do all things in Him who empowers me." In this verse to do all things does not refer to healing the sick, performing miracles, or speaking in tongues. Paul did not say that he could do all things in this way. Paul said that he could do all things to be true, honorable, righteous, pure, lovely, well-spoken of, full of virtues, and worthy of praise. Paul could do all these things in Christ who empowered him.

When reading Philippians 4:13, the wives should say, "I can do all things, including submitting myself to my husband." On the side of the husbands, the hardest thing on this earth for the husbands to do is to love their wives. It is easy to love while dating, and it is easy for the bridegroom to love the bride on the wedding day, but later on it may become difficult for the husbands to love their wives. But Paul says that we can do all things in the One who empowers us. Therefore, the husbands are able to love their wives. The sisters can be the proper wives submitting to their husbands, and the brothers can be the proper husbands loving their wives. We can do all things in Him, that is, in Christ, who empowers us. This is to live Christ.

WALKING ACCORDING TO SPIRIT

Finally, to live Christ is simply to walk according to spirit (Rom. 8:4), a mingled spirit. This spirit is the life-giving Spirit, who is Christ Himself, mingled with our regenerated spirit. There is such a mingled spirit within us. We simply need to walk so that our daily life may be according to this spirit. Confucius said that the highest learning is to cultivate the bright virtue, that is, the human conscience. But we have something much higher than the bright virtue, something much higher than the conscience. We have a mingled spirit. This mingled spirit is our regenerated human spirit indwelt by and mingled with the all-inclusive life-giving Spirit as the ultimate consummation of the processed Triune God. Now, we need to walk according to this spirit. This is to experience Christ by enjoying Him, and this is the secret of experiencing Christ.

CHAPTER EIGHT

THE SECRET OF EXPERIENCING CHRIST
IN GALATIANS

Scripture Reading: Gal. 1:4, 13-14; 2:19, 21; 4:21; 5:2-4, 17, 24; 6:13-15; 2:20; 3:2, 5, 14, 23; 4:6; 5:5-6, 16, 18, 25; 6:8, 18

Four books in the New Testament—Galatians, Ephesians, Philippians, and Colossians—may be considered the heart of the divine revelation. In recent years the Lord has shown us vision after vision and given us revelation upon revelation from these books. However, we are still short of adequate spiritual experience. This has caused me to seek a way to have more experience of Christ. Little by little, the Lord has unveiled the secret of experiencing Himself as found in these books. My burden in these chapters is not related to doctrine or even to revelation. Rather, my burden is on the secret of experiencing Christ.

THE PRESENT EVIL AGE

In order to see the secret of experiencing Christ, we need to consider the negative things Paul deals with in these books. These negative things are related to Paul's purpose in writing these Epistles.

The negative things in the book of Galatians are all part of one thing—"the present evil age." In 1:4 Paul says that Christ "gave Himself for our sins, that He might rescue us out of the present evil age." What Paul terms the present evil age is the most serious negative matter covered in Galatians. In 6:14 Paul refers to this evil age as the world: "But far be it from me to boast except in the cross of our Lord Jesus Christ, through whom the world has been crucified to me and I to the world." As the context of 6:14 makes clear, the world here is the religious world. Hence, the religious world in 6:14 is the present evil age in 1:4.

This religious world, the present evil age, includes Judaism, the law, circumcision, and tradition as four of its basic constituents. The major roles in the religious world are portrayed by the "I" and the flesh. The "I" is the fallen man, and the flesh is the expression of "I." Actually, "I" and the flesh are one. In 2:20 Paul says that the "I" has been crucified, but in 5:24 he speaks of the flesh being crucified. The cross, therefore, is the termination both of the "I" and of the flesh. The four constituents of the religious world plus the "I" and the flesh are the negative things found in the book of Galatians.

All these negative things are substitutes for Christ. In this book Paul reveals to us that Christ must now replace Judaism, the law, circumcision, and tradition. Furthermore, Christ must replace the "I" and the flesh.

According to this book, Christ is the embodiment of the Triune God. Having accomplished redemption to fulfill God's economy, Christ has become the all-inclusive Spirit, the blessing promised by God to Abraham. Such a Christ must replace all the negative things. He must be the all-inclusive replacement; He must replace our religion, law, ritual, and tradition. He must also replace our "I" and our flesh.

THE NEED TO KNOW THE SECRET

As the book of Galatians indicates, Christ has been revealed in us (1:15-16). He is living in us (2:20), and He is being formed in us (4:19). Furthermore, we have put on Christ as our clothing (3:27). Thus, Christ is not only our inner being, but He is also our outward expression. Although all this is true, we must still go on to ask how we can experience Christ moment by moment. How much do you experience in a practical way the Christ who has been revealed in you and who is now living in you? As believers, we all have received Christ, but what is the secret of applying Him continually?

Recently, I had a little problem with my health, and I tried to apply Christ to my situation. I must confess that I found it difficult to apply Him. I could sing, "Hallelujah, Christ is

Victor!" However, as soon as I stopped singing, it seemed as if Christ had vanished. I was very troubled about my difficulty in applying Christ. When I was singing hymns and praising the Lord, I could sense that Christ was Victor. But as soon as I stopped singing, I was occupied once again by thoughts of sickness. What should we do when we face such difficulties? How shall we apply Christ when our husband or wife gives us a difficult time? When we face so many hard situations in our daily living, we realize that the secret of experiencing Christ is very precious. To apply the all-inclusive Christ, the One who is so present and available, requires that we know the secret.

THE HEARING OF FAITH

A clue to the secret of experiencing Christ in Galatians is found in the phrases "in faith" and "through faith." Toward the end of 2:20 Paul says, "And the life which I now live in the flesh I live in faith, the faith of the Son of God, who loved me and gave Himself for me." Paul did not live by his own faith; he lived by the faith that is both in the Son of God and is of the Son of God. This indicates that we need to live by a certain kind of faith; however, this faith is not something that we ourselves have. Rather, it is the faith of the Son of God.

Many Bible teachers understand the word "of" in 2:20 to mean "in." But in this verse Paul speaks not of the faith *in* the Son of God, but of the faith *of* the Son of God. What we need is not only faith that is *in* Christ, but also faith that is *of* Christ. The faith is His, not ours. But we can be in this faith.

In chapter three Paul goes on to speak about the "hearing of faith." In verse 2 he inquires of the Galatian believers, "Did you receive the Spirit by the works of law or by the hearing of faith?" According to this verse, the receiving of the Spirit has much to do with the hearing of faith. In verse 5 Paul goes on to say, "He therefore who is supplying to you the Spirit and doing works of power among you, is it by the works of law or by the hearing of faith?" The supplying of the Spirit is also related to the hearing of faith. In verse 2 Paul uses the past tense, and in verse 5, the present tense. On the one hand, we received the Spirit when we believed in the Lord Jesus. This was accomplished once for all in the past. But on the other hand, the supplying of the Spirit is not once for all, but takes place continually. The hearing of faith is involved both with the receiving of the Spirit and the supplying of the Spirit. We have received the Spirit and are continually supplied with the Spirit through the hearing of faith.

What does Paul mean by faith here? If I were writing this Epistle, I would have said "by the hearing of the gospel" or "by the hearing of the word." In Romans 10:17 Paul says, "Faith comes out of hearing, and hearing through the word of Christ." In the past we have pointed out that in the New Testament faith has two aspects—the objective aspect and the subjective aspect. The objective aspect of faith includes the things in which we believe; the subjective aspect refers to our act of believing, or to our ability to believe. Although this distinction is helpful, it is not sufficient to help us know the meaning of faith in 3:2 and 5. In order to understand the meaning of faith in these verses, we need to have spiritual experiences that are very fine.

When we believed in the Lord Jesus, what we heard was not faith. Rather, what we heard was the message of the gospel, the preaching of God's word. Apart from hearing the gospel, it would not have been possible for us to have faith. Faith comes from hearing the word of God. When we preach the gospel, the good word of God, this word infuses something into those who hear. This element that is infused into others is faith. When we heard the preaching of the gospel, faith was infused into us.

THE WORD, THE SPIRIT, FAITH, AND CHRIST

Now we must go on to consider what this faith is. The faith that has been infused into us is the Spirit, and this Spirit is the word. When the word spoken to us enters into us, it becomes the Spirit, and this Spirit is the faith. According to Ephesians 2:8, we are saved by grace through faith. The faith through which we are saved is not of ourselves; it is the gift of God. Faith as a gift always comes through hearing the word. Furthermore, Hebrews 12:2 says that Christ is "the Author and Perfecter of faith." In fact, Christ Himself is our faith.

It is important that we not separate the word from the Spirit, the Spirit from faith, and faith from Christ. These four all are one. In this universe there is God. When God speaks, we have the word. As we hear the word, the Spirit is infused into us and becomes faith, a faith which is Christ Himself. When we hear the preaching of the word of God, faith is thus produced within us. In our experience, the word becomes the Spirit, the Spirit is the living faith, and this faith is Christ. The proper speaking in the meetings of the church will always produce faith in this way.

In the first two chapters of Galatians Paul speaks of Christ, but in chapter three he begins to speak of the Spirit. Through the hearing of faith we have received the Spirit. Also, the Spirit is supplied to us by the hearing of faith. This indicates the urgent need for the hearing of faith.

The hearing of faith as mentioned in 3:2 and 5 implies the word. If we do not hear the word of God, there is no way for us to have faith. Furthermore, only through the word can we apply Christ to our situation. Colossians 3:16 says, "Let the word of Christ dwell in you richly." The way to apply Christ is to contact the Word and hear the Word. As we contact the Word, the word of God comes into us and infuses us with the Spirit. Then the Spirit becomes the faith by which we live Christ and enjoy Him.

Galatians 4:6 tells us that God has sent forth the Spirit of His Son into our hearts. God sends the Spirit into our inner being through the hearing of the word. Our experience testifies of this. Whenever we pray-read and assimilate a portion of the Bible, we receive the supply of the Spirit. Then we have a living faith within us. This faith is the proper realization of Christ. With this realization we experience Christ living in us and being formed in us, and we also have the experience of being clothed with Christ.

The reason for the failures in our daily living is that we depart from the Word. I do not believe that any Christian can live in a proper way without the Bible. If we neglect the Word and pay no attention to all the verses we have heard, it will not be possible for us to live Christ. We may try to live Him, but we shall not be able to do so.

In 5:5 Paul puts the Spirit and faith together: "For we by the Spirit by faith eagerly expect the hope of righteousness." Notice that Paul first speaks of the Spirit and then of faith. If we do not have the Spirit, we cannot have faith. Faith and the Spirit are important aspects of the secret of experiencing Christ.

WALKING BY THE SPIRIT

In 5:16 and 25 Paul charges us to walk by the Spirit. If we regularly contact the Word, we shall be infused with the Spirit. This infusion of the Spirit will become the faith which is the realization of Christ. By this living faith, Christ is applied to us in our practical situations, and we experience God's salvation. In a sense, the faith produced by the infusion of the Spirit actually is our salvation. By having this faith, we become those who are in the Spirit. We should then go on to walk by the Spirit.

We need to have our daily living by the Spirit. Even in talking to our husband or wife, we should live by the Spirit. However, it is our habit to talk and do many other things apart from the Spirit. When we pray, we expect to pray by the Spirit. But in doing other things we may neglect the Spirit and be satisfied as long as the things we do are good or right. But many of the good things we do are according to our habit not according to the Spirit. As long as a certain thing is not done by the Spirit, it must be done by the "I" and by the flesh. In our daily living we do not walk absolutely by the Spirit.

As we have pointed out elsewhere, in 5:16 and 25 Paul uses two different Greek words for walk. This indicates that there are two kinds of walk by the Spirit, the walk in our daily living (v. 16) and the specific walk for the fulfillment of God's eternal purpose (v. 25). On the one hand, we need to live, walk, and have our being by the Spirit. On the other hand, we need to walk in rank, in step, by the Spirit for the fulfillment of God's purpose.

SOWING UNTO THE SPIRIT

According to Paul's word in 6:8, we also need to sow unto

the Spirit. To sow unto the Spirit is to sow with a view to the Spirit. Everything we do or say is an act of sowing. In our sowing we should aim not at the flesh, but at the Spirit. Whatever we do or say that is not with a view to the Spirit is automatically a sowing unto the flesh.

ENJOYING GRACE IN OUR SPIRIT

If through the Word we receive the Spirit and have the living faith, we shall be able to walk by the Spirit in our daily life and also have a particular walk by the Spirit for God's purpose. Moreover, we shall sow with a view to the Spirit. As a result, we shall enjoy grace. In the very last verse of Galatians Paul says, "The grace of our Lord Jesus Christ be with your spirit, brothers" (6:18). Grace is the Triune God enjoyed by us in a practical way as our portion. This enjoyment of the Triune God is in our spirit.

When we put all these matters together, we shall have the secret of experiencing Christ. We must begin by touching the Word in a living way. Through the Word we shall be infused with the Spirit. The Spirit will become in us the living faith, the realization of Christ, and we shall be one with Christ in a practical way. Following this, we need to have the two kinds of walk by the Spirit and sow with a view to the Spirit. In this way, we shall enjoy grace in our spirit.

Experiencing Christ according to all these points is a very fine matter. Neglecting this experience is like neglecting our breathing, drinking, and eating. Just as we cannot afford to neglect the things needed to maintain our physical life, so we cannot afford to neglect the Word of God. We must come to the Word and let it become in us the Spirit so that we may have faith. This faith will be to us the full realization of Christ. Then in our daily life we shall walk by the Spirit and sow unto the Spirit. Spontaneously we shall thus enjoy the Triune God as grace in our spirit. May we take this word seriously and practice it in a very fine way so that day by day and even moment by moment we may experience Christ.

CHAPTER NINE

THE SECRET OF EXPERIENCING CHRIST AND THE CHURCH IN EPHESIANS

Scripture Reading: Eph. 1:18; 2:14-15; 4:14, 17; 6:11-12; 1:13, 17; 2:8; 3:15-19; 4:23, 30; 5:18-20, 26; 6:17-18

Before we were saved, we were subject to certain negative things. According to Ephesians 2:2 and 3, these negative things included the age of this world, the ruler of the authority of the air, and the lusts of the flesh. But after we were saved, as those in Christ, as members of the church, we began to be bothered by other kinds of negative things.

SPIRITUAL BLINDNESS

According to Ephesians, the first negative thing which hinders believers is blindness. Although the word blindness is not used in the book of Ephesians, it is implied in 1:17 and 18, where Paul prays that the Father of glory would give us a spirit of wisdom and revelation in the full knowledge of Him, the eyes of our heart having been enlightened. Today millions of Christians suffer from spiritual blindness. They are blind in the eyes of their heart. This was also our situation before we came into the church life. Because we were blind, we did not know the hope of God's calling, the riches of the glory of His inheritance in the saints, and the surpassing greatness of His power toward us who believe. Furthermore, we did not know God's eternal purpose or His economy. We did not know what is meant by the all-inclusiveness of Christ, nor did we realize that the church comes into being as the fullness of the One who fills all in all through our enjoyment of the riches of Christ and participation in those riches. For the most part, we knew only that we were sinners destined for hell, but that

God loved the world and sent His Son, Jesus Christ, to die on the cross for our sins that one day we might go to heaven. We did not know the profound truths revealed in the book of Ephesians.

Preachers like to quote Paul's word in Ephesians 2:5 and 8, telling us that we are saved by grace through faith. There is even a well-known gospel song entitled "Only a Sinner Saved by Grace." According to the concept of many gospel preachers today, to be saved by grace is simply to be saved from hell. But although Ephesians 2 does speak of being saved by grace, there is no mention of hell. Rather, according to the context of this chapter, we are saved from sin, from the ruler of the authority of the air, from the course of this age, from the lustful desires of the flesh, and from death. Such a salvation makes us God's masterpiece, His workmanship (v. 10). Nevertheless, many Christians have no realization of the extent of this salvation, much less of the deeper truths concerning the Body as the fullness of Christ. In a very real sense, the eyes of many hearts have been blinded.

ORDINANCES

A second negative thing we confront after being saved is ordinances (2:15). The ordinances mentioned in Ephesians 2 refer to different ways of living and worship. As believers, we are part of the new man. However, ordinances are a hindrance to the formation of the new man. All the different nationalities have their particular ordinances, their own rituals, ways, and practices with respect to worship and daily life. The Jews have their ordinances, and the Moslems have their ways and practices. Those from the various countries in Europe have their ways, and the people in the Far East have theirs. Whenever those with different ordinances try to come together, there is friction, even enmity. How then is it possible for different peoples to become the constituents of the one new man? Humanly speaking, it is impossible. But in Ephesians 2 Paul declares that the ordinances have been nailed to the cross. This has made it possible for those of different nationalities to be one new man.

Even though the ordinances have been nailed to the cross,

they may still be very prevailing among both believers and unbelievers. Do you have the assurance that you are no longer under the influence of ordinances? If you take the time to visit believers in other countries, you will no doubt be exposed as still having certain ordinances. However, although we cannot say that we are no longer influenced by ordinances, the situation among the saints in the churches is much better now than it was several years ago. Throughout the years in the church life, we have seen the gradual disappearance of ordinances among us. But there is still the need for more improvement. Ordinances certainly are contrary to the proper experience of the church life, the Body, Christ's fullness.

WINDS OF DOCTRINE

A third negative thing in Ephesians is the winds of teaching, or the winds of doctrine (4:14). Doctrine has been a wind to blow believers away from Christ, the Head, and away from the church, the Body. Almost all Christians today are influenced by some wind of doctrine. When you meet another believer, often the first thing he will ask is what church you attend. Then he may go on to inquire about certain doctrines and teachings.

After I began the ministry in this country in 1962, I was invited to speak at different places. In almost every place I was asked questions about such doctrines as eternal security, absolute grace, baptism, and the rapture. In order not to offend those who asked, I answered very carefully. When asked about eternal security, I replied, "The best security is Christ." Regarding absolute grace, I said, "To me, no grace is more abso-lute than Christ." Likewise, concerning baptism, I answered, "The best way to be baptized is to be crucified with Christ on the cross." With respect to the rapture, I replied, "If you love the Lord and wait for Him to come back, He will certainly rapture you." These answers seemed to neutralize the doc-trinal differences and to subdue the doctrinal winds.

The wind of doctrine has distracted Christians from the proper experience of Christ. Some who have been distracted by doctrine accuse us of confusing the doctrine of the Trinity. Actually, they themselves may not believe in the Trinity, but in tritheism, in three Gods, regarding the Father as separate from the Son, and the Son as separate from the Spirit. Thus, they believe in a kind of corporate God. What heresy! By contrast, we teach the genuine Trinity in keeping with the pure Word of God. According to the Bible, God is triune; this means that He is three-one. We may say that God is three-in-one, but it is more accurate to say that He is three-one. We are not able to figure this out. We were not created with the capacity to fathom the Triune God, but we were created with the ability to receive Him.

Shortly after we moved to Anaheim, some opposing ones distributed a mimeographed paper which said that the Father, Son, and Spirit were three distinct and separate Persons. Later we put out writings saying that the three Persons are distinct, but not separate. To claim that the Father, Son, and Spirit are separate is heretical. According to the Bible, the Father and the Son cannot be separated. The Father is in the Son, and the Son is in the Father. How could it be possible to separate Them? In the light of the Bible, we believe in the co-inherence of the Three of the Godhead. We believe that the Three exist as one. Whereas we believe that the Father, Son, and Spirit co-exist mutually for eternity, many Christians teach tritheism, especially those blown about by winds of doctrine. Praise the Lord that in the local churches we are saved from the distracting winds of doctrine!

THE VANITY OF THE MIND

The fourth negative thing in Ephesians is the vanity of the mind. In 4:17 Paul says, "This therefore I say and testify in the Lord, that you no longer walk as the nations also walk in the vanity of their mind." Not only do unbelievers walk in the vanity of the mind, but even millions of today's Christians also walk in the vanity of the mind. This was the reason Paul gave the charge recorded in 4:17. In their mind unbelievers do not have God, Christ, or the Spirit; they have nothing except vanity. In the words of Solomon, apart from God everything under the sun is vanity (Eccl. 1:2). Only Christ, the embodiment of the Triune God, is reality. We must take heed not to walk in the vanity of the mind. If we would experience Christ and the church, we must be delivered from the vanity of our mind.

SATAN AND HIS EVIL POWERS

Finally, as the fifth negative element in Ephesians, we have Satan, the Devil, and his dark powers in the air. In no other book is there such an unveiling of Satan and his evil powers as in Ephesians 6. The church has a commission to fight against these powers of darkness.

OVERCOMING THE NEGATIVE THINGS

Although the gospel has been preached for more than nineteen centuries, the church still has not been built up because of these five categories of negative things— blindness, ordinances, the winds of doctrine, the vanity of the mind, and the evil powers in the air. These negative things are more serious than those in the book of Galatians. Nevertheless, in Ephesians we are given the way to overcome each of them. To overcome blindness, we need a spirit of wisdom and revelation to enlighten the eyes of our heart. To overcome ordinances we need to be strengthened with power through the Spirit into our inner man so that Christ may make His home in our hearts through faith. Then, having been rooted and grounded in love, we shall be strong to apprehend the breadth, length, height, and depth and to know the knowledge-surpassing love of Christ that we might be filled unto all the fullness of God. To overcome the winds of doctrine and the vanity of the mind, we need to be renewed in the spirit of the mind. Furthermore, there is a way for us to wrestle against the evil powers of darkness.

THE WORD, FAITH, AND THE SPIRIT

Now we must consider the secret of overcoming these negative things and of experiencing Christ and the church according to Ephesians. The secret in Ephesians is a continuation of that found in Galatians. Ephesians 1:13 is a very important verse related to this secret: "In whom you also, hearing the word of the truth, the gospel of your salvation, in whom also believing, you were sealed with the Holy Spirit of the promise." This verse speaks of hearing the word of truth, of believing in Christ, and of being sealed with the Holy Spirit. Is this not a continuation of the matter of receiving the Spirit by the hearing of faith mentioned in Galatians? In Ephesians 2:8 we see that we are saved by grace through faith. Where does this faith come from? According to 1:13, faith comes from the hearing of the Word. Hence, the first basic factor of the secret of experiencing Christ and the church is the Word.

The Word is related both to faith and to the Spirit. In our experience the Word becomes faith and Spirit. Through faith we have been saved. Moreover, according to 3:17, Christ makes His home in our hearts through faith. If we do not have this faith, there is no way for Christ to make His home in our hearts. The faith through which Christ makes His home in our hearts comes by hearing the Word and receiving the Word. As we hear the Word and receive it, something is infused into us, and this infused element becomes living faith. Therefore, if Christ is to make His home in our hearts, we need to hear the Word, deal with the Word, contact the Word, pray-read the Word, sing the Word, muse upon the Word, and dwell in the Word. The more we contact the Word in this way, the more Christ will spread into our inner being and make His home in our hearts.

RENEWED, FILLED, AND WASHED

Being renewed in the spirit of our mind also has much to do with the Word. If the Word does not enter into our mind, there is no way for the Spirit to get into our mind. But when our mind is saturated by the Word, it will be full of the Spirit. In this way the Spirit becomes the renewing Spirit in our mind.

In 5:18 Paul charges us to "be filled in spirit," no doubt with the Spirit of God. But how can the Spirit of God get into our spirit? The answer is that the Spirit comes into our spirit through the Word. When our spirit is filled with the Word, the Word, having come into us, becomes the Spirit. This is proved by 5:26 which speaks of "the washing of the water in the word." If the Word did not get into us, how could it wash us inwardly? The washing in 5:26 is not an outward washing, but a washing from within, a washing that removes spots and wrinkles, thereby accomplishing a work of transformation. If the Word could not come into us, there would be no way for the water of the Word to wash us inwardly. The fact that we are washed by the water in the Word proves that it is possible for the Word to get into us.

TAKING THE WORD BY PRAYER

In 6:17 and 18 we see the way to take in the Word: receive the Word of God by means of all prayer and petition. When we receive the Word by prayer and petition, the Word gets into us and becomes the Spirit who fills our spirit and spreads into our mind, becoming the Spirit of the mind and renewing the mind. Furthermore, the Word washes us inwardly and, by spreading into the inward parts of our being, makes a home for Christ within us. Therefore, this matter of the Word is a line that goes from 1:13 to 6:17 and 18.

THE RESULT OF TAKING THE WORD
IN A PROPER WAY

If we read and pray-read the Bible in a proper way, even musing upon the Word, singing it, and dwelling in it, our inner being will be filled. We may say that we are filled with the Word, with the Spirit, or with faith. We may also say that we are filled with the anointing, with God, or with Christ. By this inward filling we have the power to defeat the darkness in the air. We also have the living water flowing within us to wash away the old elements, the wrinkles and the spots, and to renew us. When we are filled in this way, we sense that Christ is settling Himself in our being, making our inner chambers the rooms for His dwelling place. Also, when we enjoy such a filling, we love all believers, no matter what their nationality may be. Moreover, our inner eyes are enlightened, and our vision becomes clear.

Before we learned to take the Word in this way, we were blind, empty, weak, and full of oldness. We had no way to deal with the evil powers in the air. But now by taking the Word in the proper way, reading it, pray-reading it, and even singing and praising with it, we are filled inwardly and have the power to defeat Satan. Oh, there is nothing more refreshing and cleansing than to be inwardly washed by the water in the Word! When we are filled with the Word and washed by it, our entire being is renewed and transparent, and we have a foretaste of the New Jerusalem. At such a time we do not care for doctrine; we care only for Christ and His Body. Furthermore, the universal dimensions of Christ and His knowledge-surpassing love become our experience. We are saturated with Christ and one with Christ. As a result, we become Christ's home, and we love all the saints in the church life, both the young and the old. If we all are filled inwardly by contacting the Word in a proper way, the young ones will love the older ones, and the older ones will love the young ones. When an older saint sees a teenager standing up to praise the Lord, his heart will leap for joy. In our experience we shall know that all ordinances have been abolished. From my experience I can testify that this truly is the secret of enjoying Christ and participating in the church life.

THE NEED TO PERSEVERE

We need more prayer and petition to receive the Word of God. According to 6:17 and 18, we need to pray at every time in spirit. When we pray, there is no need for us to compose our own prayers; we have the Bible as our prayer book. The best way to pray is to pray with the Word of God. As we pray the Word, we must exercise our spirit and thereby take the Word by means of prayer. Then we shall enjoy Christ and participate in the church life. We need to watch unto this prayer and persevere in it all day long. Although the powers of darkness may try to quench us and keep us from praying this way, we need to persevere and continue to pray with the Word by exercising our spirit. If we practice this, we shall enjoy the secret revealed in Ephesians. Then we shall have the proper experience of Christ and the church.

CHAPTER TEN

THE SECRET OF EXPERIENCING CHRIST IN PHILIPPIANS

Scripture Reading: Phil. 1:17, 20; 2:3a, 4, 14, 21; 3:2, 4-8; 4:6a, 11; 1:19-21a; 2:12b-13, 16a; 3:3, 8b-9a; 4:4, 6b, 13, 23

Before we consider the secret of experiencing Christ according to the book of Philippians, I would like to say a further word about the secret as seen in Ephesians.

THE WORD, FAITH, AND THE SPIRIT

Ephesians 1:13 is a crucial verse: "In whom you also, hearing the word of the truth, the gospel of your salvation, in whom also believing, you were sealed with the Holy Spirit of the promise." This verse speaks of hearing the word of truth, of believing in Christ, and of being sealed with the Holy Spirit. Hence, three things—the Word, faith, and the Spirit—are implied here. Without the Word, there can be no faith, no believing. Faith comes through the Word. If we did not have the Bible or the preaching of the gospel, it would not be possible to have faith. According to the Bible, Abraham is the father of those who believe. In Galatians 3:8 Paul says, "And the Scripture, foreseeing that God would justify the nations by faith, preached the gospel beforehand to Abraham." Because God preached the gospel to him, Abraham could believe. However, had there been no speaking of God, Abraham could not have believed. Faith is the result of God's spoken word infused into those who hear the Word. From our experience we can testify that if we had not heard the gospel or read the Bible, we could not have faith.

During the early years of my ministry, I did a great deal of gospel preaching. Often after a meeting, people would come to me for help. Instead of explaining a lot to them, I preferred to have them read a verse, perhaps John 3:16. First I would read the verse aloud and then ask the others to read it one by one. At that time, I did not practice pray-reading, but I did know the effectiveness of repeating the Word of God. After having the seeking ones repeat a verse, I often asked them to insert their name at the appropriate places. For example, I would have them insert their name as we were reading John 3:16. Through reading the Word in such a way, many received faith and were saved.

Receiving faith through the Word is not a matter of psychology. On the contrary, this has much to do with the Spirit. Wherever the Word of God is preached, the Spirit of God is present. The Lord Jesus once said, "The words which I have spoken unto you are spirit and are life" (John 6:63). In the light of this verse, we believe that God's Word is Spirit. Believing this, we need to present the Word of God to others in a living way, encouraging them not simply to read it with the mind, but to take it in by an exercise of heart and spirit. Whenever the Word is taken in this way, spontaneously something rises up in a person which causes him to believe in God. This is faith.

When faith rises up, the Spirit is present also. We cannot separate faith from the Spirit. Actually, faith is a function of the Spirit. When we read the Word in a proper way and the Word is infused into us, it becomes the Spirit. Then the Spirit functions to produce faith. Faith, therefore, is the result of the function of the Spirit.

The Spirit enters into our being, especially into our spirit, through the Word. We may even say that the Spirit comes in as the Word. When we handle the Word of God rightly, the Word will enter into us and become the Spirit functioning in us to give us faith. Then in our experience we shall have the hearing of the Word, the believing in Christ, and the receiving of the Spirit.

Preachers of the gospel often use Ephesians 2:5 and 8 to tell people that we are saved by grace through faith. But many who use these verses in preaching the gospel may not realize that the faith through which we are saved comes from the Word with the Spirit. Saving faith is produced by the infusion of the living Word with the Spirit. This kind of faith is not a mere doctrinal faith; it is a living faith that comes from the Word with the Spirit.

THE CONTINUAL EXPERIENCE
OF GOD'S SALVATION

Although we have the assurance that we are eternally saved, we still need to be saved day by day and even moment by moment. For this continual experience of God's salvation, we need the Word, faith, and the Spirit. These three elements are like a threefold cord. By this threefold cord, constituted of the Word, the Spirit, and faith, we are saved from all the negative things in Ephesians: blindness, ordinances, winds of doctrine, vanity of the mind, and Satan and his evil powers of darkness. Furthermore, it is by the Word with the Spirit producing faith that we receive a spirit of wisdom and revelation and are enlightened. This is also the way for Christ to spread Himself throughout our inner being and to settle, make His home, in our hearts. According to Ephesians 3:17, Christ makes His home in our hearts through faith. Moreover, when our mind is saturated with the Word, the Spirit spreads into our mind, and we are renewed in the spirit of the mind.

FILLED, WASHED, ARMED, AND EMPOWERED

By the Word with the Spirit we are also filled in our spirit. Ephesians 5:18-20 speaks of being filled in spirit, speaking, singing, psalming, and giving thanks. If we compare this passage with Colossians 3:16 and 17, we see that the Spirit fills us through the Word. Hence, to be filled with the Word is actually to be filled with the Spirit.

By the Word coming into our being and filling it, we are also washed; we are cleansed by the washing of water in the Word (Eph. 5:26). According to the New Testament, this water, the water in the Word, is the living Spirit. When we receive the Word into us, the water in the Word will wash away our inward filthiness.

According to Ephesians 6:17 and 18, if we receive the Word into our being by means of prayer and petition, we shall put on the armor of God and be empowered. Apart from the Word, there is no way for us to have the armor of God. To put on the armor of God is to receive the Word by means of all prayer and petition. Our experience confirms this. When we come to the Word and take it into us by pray-reading, singing, or musing, we eventually sense that we are armed, equipped, and empowered. We have the confidence that should Satan attack us we would have the power and the armor to defeat him. We can even say, "Satan, don't you see that I have put on the armor of God and that I have been empowered to defeat you and to put you to shame?" We are thus able to fight the spiritual warfare and defeat the evil powers of darkness in the air.

ENJOYING CHRIST AND THE CHURCH

By the Word with the Spirit producing faith we experience Christ and the church life. According to your experience, when do you have the highest enjoyment of Christ and the church? Is it not when you take the Word into your being through the Spirit by praying in spirit? When we pray-read the Word, we receive the Word not merely into our mind, but also into our spirit. Then in our experience Christ becomes available, present, and real, and we rejoice to be in the church life.

Ephesians 6 speaks of taking the Word by praying at every time in spirit. In order to do this in a practical way, it is good to carry a pocket version of the New Testament with you. Should you be delayed in heavy traffic on the way home from work, you can open this pocket version and pray-read a verse. Even in the midst of a traffic jam you can enjoy pray-reading a verse like Philippians 2:9: "God highly exalted Him and bestowed on Him the name which is above every name."

If a brother pray-reads the Word on the way home from work, he will be happy with his wife. How different this is from coming home exhausted and finding his wife worn out from the day's labor! When a brother and his wife are exhausted and not enjoying the Word, neither is likely to be happy in the Lord. At such a time, it seems that Christ has disappeared, and there is no incentive or desire for the church life.

The secret of experiencing Christ and the church is in the Word. When we take the Word in a proper way, we experience Christ and enjoy the church life. We may even feel like singing, "Unto Him be glory in the church." Whenever we enjoy Christ and the church in this way, Satan, the Devil, is under our feet.

NEGATIVE THINGS IN PHILIPPIANS

Compared with those in Galatians and Ephesians, the negative things in Philippians are small matters. Instead of such things as the religious world, ordinances, the vanity of the mind, and Satan, we have murmurings, reasonings, rivalry, vainglory, and anxiety.

Rivalry

Certain ones, especially the Judaizers, were in rivalry with Paul. They were those who announced Christ "out of rivalry, not purely" (1:17). There is also rivalry among Christians today. Recently I heard that a certain Christian friend of mine, whom I have known for more than twenty years, said, "Witness Lee's ministry is spreading throughout the earth. We must stop him!" Such a statement comes out of rivalry.

Rivalry gives rise to persecution, and persecution causes affliction. According to Paul's word in 1:17, those who announce Christ out of rivalry thought "to raise up affliction in my bonds." Their intention was to increase Paul's afflictions. Nevertheless, even though Paul was suffering, he was not defeated by his afflictions. He could say, "According to my earnest expectation and hope that in nothing I shall be put to shame, but with all boldness, as always, even now Christ shall be magnified in my body, whether through life or through death" (1:20).

In 2:3 Paul exhorts the saints to do "nothing by way of rivalry nor by way of vainglory, but in lowliness of mind counting one another more excellent than yourselves." Do not think that in the church today there is no rivalry for vainglory. When a brother hears a certain person ministering the Word in a rich way, he may say to himself, "Wait for a few years, and

I will surprise you with my rich speaking. My speaking will be much better than this." This is an example of the rivalry for vainglory which may be hidden within you.

In 2:4 Paul goes on to say, "Not regarding each his own things, but each the things of others also." The things here denote virtues and qualities. We should not regard only our own virtues and qualities, but those of others also. Instead of thinking so much about our own virtues, qualities, abilities, and attainments, we should regard the things of others. In keeping with Paul's word, we should even count others more excellent than ourselves. As we consider others in the church, we should think of them as better than ourselves.

Murmurings and Reasonings

In 2:14 Paul says, "Do all things without murmurings and reasonings." Elsewhere I have pointed out that murmurings, which are of the emotion, are found mostly among the sisters, whereas reasonings, which are of the mind, are found mostly among the brothers. However, I sometimes have problems with both murmurings and reasonings. I may murmur inwardly over the small portion of food my wife may serve me at dinner, especially when I compare my portion with that of others. I also may reason inwardly when my wife points out that a certain food is good for me and that I need to eat it. Do you not also have problems with the "bugs" of murmurings and reasonings? We all are bothered by these things.

Seeking Our Own Things

In 2:21 Paul says that "all seek their own things, not the things of Christ Jesus." The phrase "their own things" here refers not to virtues and qualities as in 2:4, but to our personal affairs. We may care for our personal affairs and not for the things of Christ. Probably you have not realized that personal affairs are a negative thing keeping you from the experience of Christ. However, you may actually care more for your domestic affairs than for Christ, more for your education or employment than for the church life. But of Timothy Paul could say that he would "genuinely care for what concerns" the church, whereas others cared for their own things, not the things of Christ. If we go on caring for our own things instead of caring for the things of Christ, there will be no way to have the church life.

Dogs, Evil Workers, the Concision

In 3:2 Paul issues a serious charge: "Beware of the dogs, beware of the evil workers, beware of the concision." Those who were dogs, evil workers, the concision, held to certain religious concepts which were troubling to the saints and were a source of distraction from Christ. In dealing with such people we should care for one basic principle: Does this person's word help us to experience Christ and to have more of the church life, or does it distract us from Christ and the church? If it does not encourage us to experience Christ and to live the church life, we should pay no attention to it. That person must be a dog, an evil worker, one who contemptuously follows certain religious rituals (the meaning of the term concision). Instead of trying to determine whether the word of such a person is right or wrong, ask if his speaking helps you to enjoy Christ or distracts you from Christ, if it encourages you to have more of the church life or keeps you away from the church. If it turns you away from Christ and the church, it is the speech of one who is a dog, an evil worker, a member of the concision, and one who should be avoided.

Confidence in the Flesh

In 3:4-8 Paul goes on to deal with yet another negative thing—confidence in the flesh. Verse 4 says, "Though I myself could have confidence also in the flesh; if any other man thinks to have confidence in the flesh, I more." In these verses confidence in the flesh refers to all the good items or qualities we have in the flesh. For Paul, these included circumcision on the eighth day and being a Hebrew of the Hebrews. For us today, they may include pride in our nationality or culture. Such confidence in the flesh keeps us from Christ and frustrates the church life.

Anxiety

Another negative thing found in Philippians is anxiety. In

4:6 Paul says, "In nothing be anxious." To be anxious is to worry. It is very difficult for people who are cautious and sensitive not to have anxiety. Many years ago there was a fire in the place where I worked, and later, a burglary. This caused me to be anxious, to be filled with worry over the threat of fire and theft. As a sensitive person, it is easy for me to have this kind of anxiety.

I have prayed over Paul's word about anxiety many times. I have said, "Lord, I thank You for this word. This is not only Your commandment, but also Your promise. Lord, I take Your word and ask You to save me from anxiety." But the more I prayed in this way, the more anxious I became. How difficult it is to be free from anxiety! Anxiety is a very irritating "mosquito." It seems that the only ones who have no anxiety are those who are careless about life. Their attitude seems to be, "Life is in the hands of God. There is no need to worry about it." This, however, is not true faith, but the expression of a natural indifference. Those who are careless may have no anxiety, but every sensitive and cautious person suffers a great deal of anxiety.

Want

The last of the negative things in Philippians is what Paul describes as want (4:11). To be in want is to have a material need. Being short of the supply to meet a material or financial need may be a cause of serious concern. Such circumstances certainly are a negative thing which needs to be overcome.

THE BOUNTIFUL SUPPLY AND THE WORD OF LIFE

In 1:19 Paul says, "For I know that for me this shall turn out to salvation through your petition and the bountiful supply of the Spirit of Jesus Christ." Then in verses 20 and 21 he speaks of magnifying Christ and of living Christ. To live Christ and magnify Him requires the bountiful supply of the Spirit of Jesus Christ. But how can this bountiful supply be applied to us? The secret of experiencing this bountiful supply is in holding forth the word of life (2:16). As Paul was living Christ and magnifying Him, he was no doubt holding forth the word of life. This was the reason that even some among Caesar's household could be saved. They realized that Paul, a prisoner there in Rome, was holding forth the word of life. Paul's word in 2:16 indicates that the bountiful supply of the Spirit was applied to him because he was receiving the word of life.

From Ephesians 1:13 we have seen that the Spirit is inseparable from the Word and comes with the Word. If there is no Word, there can be no Spirit. But when there is the preaching of the Word, it will be possible for those who hear this preaching to receive the Spirit. Paul received the word of life. When the word of life entered into him, it became the bountiful supply of the Spirit which enabled him to magnify Christ and live Him.

In Philippians 1:20 Paul speaks of magnifying Christ and in 2:16, of holding forth the word of life. Actually, Christ is the word of life, and the word of life is Christ. Furthermore, in 2:13 Paul says that God operates in us "both the willing and the working for His good pleasure." Yes, it is God who works in us and operates in us. But when this operating God is expressed, He is the word of life.

Unless we receive the word of life into our being, we shall not be able to hold forth this word, to magnify it, to manifest it. How can we magnify the word of life if the word has not come into us to be magnified? In order to hold forth the word of life, we must first receive the word of life into us. Take eating as an illustration. If a person does not eat properly for several days, his face will not have a healthy color. But if he daily receives a nourishing supply of food, his complexion will be healthy. It will be the expression of the nourishing food he has eaten, digested, and assimilated. The principle is the same with holding forth the word of life. The secret is to handle the Word in a proper way and thereby to receive the Spirit. The Spirit will then function in us as our living faith. In this way we shall overcome rivalry, vainglory, murmurings, reasonings, our own things, anxiety, and want. Then we shall be able to say with Paul, "I can do all things in Him who empowers me" (4:13).

Christ empowers us through the Word. Suppose you neglect the Word for several days. Will you still be empowered by Christ? Certainly not! Food empowers you only when you eat of it. Likewise, Christ empowers you only when you take the Word into your being. By taking in the divine element through the Word, we are empowered. Then we can do all things in Him who empowers us through the Word.

Paul concludes the Epistle to the Philippians by saying, "The grace of the Lord Jesus Christ be with your spirit." It is important to realize that whatever we enjoy by receiving the Word eventually becomes the grace in our spirit. Once again we see that we need to contact the Word and receive it by prayer, exercising our spirit to pray-read the Word in order to be supplied with the Spirit. Receiving the Spirit through the Word, we shall have the faith to receive grace as our enjoyment. Then we shall have the experience of Christ with the enjoyment of the church life.

CHAPTER ELEVEN

THE SECRET OF EXPERIENCING CHRIST, THE HEAD, FOR THE CHURCH, THE BODY

Scripture Reading: Col. 2:4, 8, 16-18, 20-23; 3:2b; 1:8, 24; 2:5-7; 3:2a, 16, 17; 4:2

NEGATIVE THINGS

In Colossians 2:8 Paul mentions some of the negative things dealt with in this book: "Beware that no one carries you off as spoil through his philosophy and empty deceit, according to the tradition of men, according to the elements of the world, and not according to Christ." Here Paul speaks of philosophy, tradition, and the elements of the world. In 2:23 he refers to asceticism when he speaks of "self-imposed worship and humility and severe treatment of the body." According to 2:8, philosophy is involved with tradition and the elements of the world. Self-imposed ascetic practices have much to do with tradition.

Every group of people has its own particular elements of the world, or elementary teachings. Wherever the gospel is preached, those who proclaim the gospel will confront elementary teachings, certain traditions, and philosophies. Both modern, scientific countries and undeveloped countries have their own elementary teachings, elements of the world.

Philosophy, tradition, asceticism, and the various elements of the world are the negative things found in the book of Colossians. I do not have the assurance that the saints in the Lord's recovery have been thoroughly and absolutely rescued from the elements of the world and from the "commandments and teachings of men" (Col. 2:22).

As one born in China, I studied the classical writings of

Confucius and was influenced somewhat by his philosophical teachings. But now I can testify before the Lord and before all the angels that I am no longer under the influence of any philosophical things. This influence has been swallowed up by the Bible. I have been reading the Word for more than fifty years. As a result, in my inner being there is no influence of any kind of philosophy. The only influence on my inward constituent is the Bible. This is the reason that I am able to enjoy Christ.

THE WORD OF CHRIST

In 3:16 Paul says, "Let the word of Christ dwell in you richly." The way to be delivered from the negative things found in the book of Colossians is to let the word of Christ dwell in us, to inhabit us, richly. If the word of Christ is to dwell in us richly, it is not sufficient for us to read the Bible only on occasion or even three or four times a week. On the contrary, we need to take the word of the Bible as our daily food, our daily manna. In fact, just as we eat three meals a day, it is best to feed on the Word three times a day. Then the ingredients of the Word will enter into us and be constituted into our very being.

GOD AND THE WORD

When we take in the Word in a proper way, we have both faith and the Spirit. In a very real sense, the Word, the Spirit, and faith are one. At least they are of one source, and that source is God.

As the unique source, God is the Word. "In the beginning was the Word...and the Word was God" (John 1:1). Have you ever realized that the greatest wonder in the universe is the Word of God? Creation, redemption, regeneration, sanctification, and transformation all take place by the Word. If God had been silent—that is, if there had been no Word—there could have been no creation. Creation came about through God's speaking. When God spoke, all the items of creation came into being. How marvelous that our God is a speaking God! This speaking God is the Word. Regarding this, John 1:1 is a strategic verse, for this verse declares that the Word was God. If we had written the Gospel of John, instead of "In the beginning was the Word," we might have said, "In the beginning was God." But at the opening of the Gospel of John, John puts the Word before God. Some readers may think that John was mistaken in doing this. Who is the source, God or the Word? There can be no doubt that God is the source. Why, then, did John put the Word first? Why did John not say, "In the beginning was God, and God was the Word"? The reason John put the Word first is that nothing comes into existence apart from the Word. It was through the Word that all things have come into being. The entire Gospel of John is built upon the Word. Furthermore, the church life is founded on the Word. If we had not heard the preaching of the Word of God, we could not have been saved and regenerated, and we could not have become a part of the Body of Christ. The Word is the source of re-creation as well as of creation.

THE WORD, FAITH, AND THE SPIRIT

According to the New Testament, whenever we hear the Word, faith is produced within us. Faith is a marvelous thing; no one can fully explain it. When I was young, I heard a preacher define faith by saying that faith is like the assurance a member of a political party has that the policy of that party will be a success in practice. This may be a definition of secular faith or worldly faith, but it has nothing to do with the faith spoken of in the New Testament. We simply are not able to define adequately what genuine faith is. But by our experience we know that when we come to the Bible in a proper way and repeat a certain verse, we are inspired, and faith is produced within us. The more we repeat a portion of the Word of God, the more we are inspired. There is no true inspiration, however, in repeating the words of Plato, Confucius, or any other philosopher.

The Bible is inspiring because it is the Word of life, the living Word. It is living because it is the expression of the living God. According to John 1:1, the Word is God. According to John 6:63, the words spoken by the Lord Jesus are spirit and life. Thus, the Word is both God and the Spirit. John 4:24 says, "God is Spirit." The Bible reveals that it is impossible to separate the Word, God, Christ, and the Spirit. The Word is God, Christ, and the Spirit.

When we read the Bible in a proper way, especially when we pray-read it, we receive inspiration. This inspiration is the moving of the living Spirit within us. This moving of the Spirit is the function of the Spirit, and in the New Testament this function is called faith. Faith is always intimately related to the Word and the Spirit. Whenever we read of faith in the New Testament, we should realize that both the Word and the Spirit are implied. For example, Ephesians 3:17 says, "That Christ may make His home in your hearts through faith." The phrase "through faith" implies the Word and the Spirit. The same is true of Ephesians 2:8, which says that we are saved by grace through faith. The faith through which we are saved is the faith that implies the Word and the Spirit. In Colossians 2:5 Paul speaks of "the firmness of your faith in Christ," and in verse 7, of "being established in the faith." In these verses also faith implies the Word and the Spirit.

If we did not have the Word, we could not have the Spirit. Likewise, if we did not have the Word and the Spirit, there would be no way for us to have faith. But when we are filled with the Word, we are automatically filled with the Spirit. Then we are spontaneously filled also with faith.

When I was young, I often heard Christians talking about faith. I began to pray that the Lord would give me a strong faith. But the more I prayed for faith, the less faith I had. Gradually I learned that the way to have faith is not just to pray for it, but to take in the Word in a proper way. By reading the Word again and again, my faith was strengthened.

Brother Nee encouraged us to take a few verses every morning and repeat them and muse upon them. When I did this, I found that I had faith spontaneously. As I look back on my experience, I realize that I had not only faith, but also the inner sense that I had been filled with the Spirit. Thus, from our experience we know that when we have the living Word in us, we also have the Spirit and faith.

The four books of Galatians, Ephesians, Philippians, and Colossians all speak of the Word, the Spirit, and faith. In Galatians, the emphasis is on faith; in Ephesians, on the Spirit;

and in Colossians, on the Word. In Philippians the emphasis is on all three. According to Galatians, faith comes from hearing the Word. Although Ephesians strongly emphasizes the Spirit, the Spirit is mentioned only once in Colossians, in 1:8, where Paul speaks of the saints' love in the Spirit. Philippians speaks of both the bountiful supply of the Spirit and also of the word of life (1:19; 2:16). In Ephesians the Word is called the word of God (6:17); in Philippians, the word of life; and in Colossians, the word of Christ (3:16). Again and again I wish to point out the fact that apart from the Word we cannot have the Spirit or faith.

If we would enjoy Christ and experience Him, we must have the Spirit, and we must also have faith. Without the Spirit, how can we experience Christ? And without faith, what way do we have to enjoy Christ? If we would have the Spirit and the faith to experience Christ and enjoy Him, we must come to the Word again and again. Faith and the Spirit are found in no place other than the Word. The more we get into the Word, the better. The Christian life is a life that is continually dealing with the divine Word. The Word must be before our eyes, in our spirit, in our heart, in our mind, in our mouth, and on our lips. Our whole being must be saturated with the Word of God. When the Word is outside us, it is simply the Word. But when the Word enters into us, it becomes the Spirit who gives us the faith to enjoy Christ and experience Him.

EXERCISING THE SPIRIT TO PRAY-READ THE WORD

The books of Galatians, Ephesians, Philippians, and Colossians all have a particular emphasis. But if we put these books together, we see five things that are crucial for our experience of Christ: the Word, faith, the Spirit, our spirit, and prayer. If God had not created us with a spirit, we would not be able to receive inspiration from the Word, no matter how many times we may read it or repeat parts of it. The inspiration which comes from the Word is not a matter of emotion. Human words may touch our emotion, but they do not touch our spirit. I studied the classical writings of Confucius, but none of those writings touched my spirit. Certain writings may stir our emotions, but only the Word of God can inspire our spirit. Only one book—the Bible—is able to touch our spirit. According to Hebrews 4:12, the Word of God is a sharp sword that even divides soul from spirit.

John 4:24 says that God is Spirit and that those who worship Him must worship Him in spirit. In worshipping God it is best to deal with His Word. But when we read the Word, we should use not only our eyes and our mind, but especially our spirit. When many Christians read the Bible, they just read with their eyes and try to understand with their mentality. They stop short of allowing the Word to touch their spirit. If we want the Word to touch our spirit, we should pray-read the Word.

Before we began to practice pray-reading, I would often pray after reading two or three verses. Having read these verses, I would ask the Lord to make them my experience. Although this practice is helpful, it is not as helpful as pray-reading. In pray-reading the Word, there is no need to wait until we have finished reading before we pray. Instead, we read by praying, mingling our reading with prayer. Then we receive the Word of God by means of all prayer and petition.

Colossians 3:16 charges us to let the word of Christ dwell in us richly. If we would let the word of Christ dwell in us, we need to receive the Word by means of all prayer. According to the Bible, the ultimate way to receive the Word is to pray it. Let us use Philippians 3:17 as an illustration: "Be imitators together of me, brothers, and observe attentively those who thus walk as you have us for an example." You may be inspired by reading this verse. But only when you pray will this word get into you. How good it is to take such a verse into us by prayer! When we pray-read the Word, the Word does not stay in our mouth, but enters into our inner being. This is to receive the Word by means of prayer. As we pray the Word, the Word enters into the very depths of our being.

As an elderly man with many years of experience, I can testify that the best way to take the Word is by means of all prayer. By praying the Word we drink the living water in the Word. Then this living water fills our inner being and causes us to be nourished and healthy. In 1 Timothy 6:3 and

2 Timothy 1:13 Paul uses the expression "healthy words." When we pray-read the Word, the Word becomes to us the healthy Word. By this healthy Word we experience Christ.

We thank the Lord that He created us with a spirit by which we may drink His Word. But if we would use our spirit to drink the Word, we need to exercise the spirit. The best way to exercise our spirit is to pray. Ephesians 6:17 and 18 say that we should receive the Word of God by means of all prayer, praying at every time in spirit. If we would have the Word, faith, and the Spirit, we need to exercise our spirit by praying. When we walk, we automatically exercise our feet. Likewise, when we pray, we spontaneously exercise our spirit. Paul charges us to pray at every time (Eph. 6:18) and also to persevere in prayer (Col. 4:2). If we want to enjoy the Word and have the Spirit with faith, we must pray by exercising our spirit.

THE DIVINE SPIRIT AND THE HUMAN SPIRIT

In Colossians 2:5 Paul says, "For though indeed I am absent in the flesh, yet in the spirit I am with you, rejoicing and seeing your order and the firmness of your faith in Christ." This verse indicates that Paul was a person who lived in the spirit. When he wrote this word to the Colossians, he was far away from them. Nevertheless, he could say that he was with them in spirit, rejoicing and seeing their order and the firmness of their faith in Christ. In his spirit Paul had a heavenly telescope through which he could see the situation of the saints in Colossae. He knew that they were in order and that their faith was firm.

In Colossians Paul speaks of the divine Spirit (1:8) and the human spirit (2:5). This indicates that in order to experience Christ, we need these two spirits. As we have pointed out, we also need to persevere in prayer. The secret of experiencing Christ has much to do with the Word, the Spirit, faith, the human spirit, and prayer.

RELEASING THE EXPERIENCE OF CHRIST
TO THE BODY

In the book of Colossians Paul covers not only the secret of experiencing Christ, the Head, but also the secret of experiencing the church, the Body. We need to know the secret of experiencing the Head for the Body. In 1:24 Paul says, "Now I rejoice in my sufferings on your behalf, and fill up that which is lacking of the afflictions of Christ in my flesh for His Body, which is the church." The fact that Paul suffered for the Body indicates that whatever we experience of Christ must be for the Body. If we do not supply the Body with our experience of Christ, our experience will be terminated. Consider your physical body: every member of your body enjoys the circulation of the blood. However, if the blood flowed into your arm and stayed there, not continuing to circulate through the rest of the body, that would be a sign of serious trouble. Your whole body would be in great danger. This illustration shows that we should not keep our experience of Christ for ourselves, but use it to supply the Body. The ultimate issue of our experience of Christ must be for the Body.

During my years in Christianity, I did not hear anything about the experience of Christ. Neither was I told that we need to receive grace from the Lord and then transmit this grace to other members of the Body. We definitely need to exercise our spirit by prayer to receive the Word so that we may have the Spirit and faith to experience Christ and enjoy Him. But what we receive of Christ must then be released to the Body. We should not hold it for ourselves. Our spiritual blood vessels need to be enlarged to allow the life supply to pass through us to others. Do not keep the supply for yourself. If you do this, you will have serious difficulties. Come to the church meetings and release your experience of Christ.

The more we release, the more supply we shall have. This is why I am not exhausted by ministering the Word. On the contrary, speaking always supplies me with more spiritual riches. As the flow goes out, more comes in. In fact, the inflow depends on the outflow. The more we release, the more we are able to take in. The more we release for the Body, the more supply we shall receive for the Body. The Word, the Spirit, faith, our spirit, and our prayer must all be for the Body. Release Christ and release the spirit for the Body. Do not come to the meetings to sit in silence, but come to release your experience of Christ to the Body.

CARING FOR OTHERS

In our daily life we also need to care for the younger ones, sharing with them our experience of Christ and enjoyment of Him. The Christian life is a Body life, a life of mutuality. You take care of other members, and others take care of you. On the one hand, you receive the supply; on the other hand, you return it by taking care of others.

PRAYING FOR ALL THE SAINTS

According to Ephesians and Colossians, we must also pray for all the saints (Eph. 6:18; Col. 4:2). Every member of the Body needs prayer. Do not think that a particular member is so strong that he does not need you to pray for him. Every member of the Body needs the prayers of the other members. You need me, and I need you. We all need to pray for all the saints. By functioning in the meetings, caring for the younger ones, and praying for all the saints, we shall release the riches of the Christ we have experienced to the other members in the Body.

SHARING THE MATERIAL SUPPLY

Finally, the material supply we gain through the Lord's blessing should also be shared with the Body. We should consider our income to be not only for our personal use and for our family, but also for the Body. In the book of Philippians Paul indicates that this sharing of material supply is for the furtherance of the gospel. As such, it is part of the fellowship of the gospel (1:5; 4:14-15) to use material things for the Body of Christ.

Our concern should be for the Body universally. I can testify that I am very burdened for the churches in Africa. In particular, the church in Accra, Ghana, is in desperate need of a meeting hall. There is no way for them to build a meeting hall themselves. Saints in other parts of the world should take up the burden to help them. This is not to raise funds for a Christian activity. Rather, it is to release to the Lord's Body what we have received from Him both spiritually and materially. If we do this, we shall have a rich experience of Christ for the Body.